GOD AND TWO POETS

Other books by the author:

Action, Emotion and Will (1963)
Descartes (1968)
The Five Ways (1969)
Wittgenstein (1973)
The Anatomy of the Soul (1974)
Will, Freedom and Power (1975)
The Aristotelian Ethics (1978)
Freewill and Responsibility (1978)
Aristotle's Theory of the Will (1979)
The God of the Philosophers (1979)
Aquinas (1980)
The Computation of Style (1982)
Faith and Reason (1983)
Thomas More (1983)
The Legacy of Wittgenstein (1984)
The Logic of Deterrence (1985)
The Ivory Tower (1985)
Wyclif (1985)
A Stylometric Study of the New Testament (1986)
The Road to Hillsborough (1986)
Reason and Religion (1987)
The Heritage of Wisdom (1987)

GOD AND TWO POETS

*Arthur Hugh Clough and
Gerard Manley Hopkins*

ANTHONY KENNY

SIDGWICK & JACKSON
LONDON

First published in Great Britain in 1988
by Sidgwick & Jackson Limited

Copyright © 1988 by Anthony Kenny

ISBN 0 283 99387 1

Photoset by Rowland Phototypesetting Limited
Bury St Edmunds, Suffolk
Printed in Great Britain by Adlard and Son Limited
Dorking, Surrey, and Letchworth, Hertfordshire
for Sidgwick & Jackson Limited
1 Tavistock Chambers, Bloomsbury Way
London WC1A 2SG

To Nancy

ACKNOWLEDGEMENTS

I am grateful to Graham Greene and Dan Davin who first introduced me to the poetry of Clough; and to Roger Lonsdale, Peter
Hinchcliff and Carl Schmidt, who answered many ignorant
queries.

I am indebted to the Oxford University Press for permission to
make use of texts in the 1974 edition of Clough's poems and the
Oxford Authors volume on Hopkins.

I am much obliged to the staff of Sidgwick & Jackson, and in
particular to Carey Smith, for the care they have taken in publishing
this book.

CONTENTS

PROLOGUE

In 1951 there appeared the first modern edition of the poems of Arthur Hugh Clough. A decade later, Katherine Chorley could introduce a biography of Clough as follows:

> In the *Oxford Book of Victorian Verse*, Arthur Hugh Clough is represented by four short poems and an excerpt of half a dozen lines. Everyone knows two of these poems, *Say not the Struggle* and the *Latest Decalogue*, but most casual readers of poetry leave it at that and would be hard put to it to quote any of his other poems. Yet these examples are only like thin branches cut off from the great boughs and trunk of his poetry.
>
> (Chorley: 1)

In the eight years after Chorley's book was published there was a great revival of interest in Clough; five full-length studies were published by 1970. Oddly enough, this Clough renaissance came to an end when the second, much enlarged edition of his *Poems* appeared in 1974. Since that time, comparatively little has been written about him in all the flood of writing about Victorian poets.

Now there are signs of a new revival of interest. The *New Oxford Book of Victorian Verse*, edited by Christopher Ricks, devotes some forty pages to Clough, and includes one of his longest poems, the epistolary novel in verse called *Amours de Voyage*. The approach of the centenary of the death of Matthew Arnold in 1988 has reminded scholars also of the poet who was Arnold's great friend and for whom Arnold provided a remarkable epitaph in his poem *Thyrsis*.

This book is a study of Clough's religious thought, as expressed in his prose and verse. Because it concentrates on his religious verse, it will leave out of account many of the finest things he wrote, including the greater part of *Amours de Voyage* which would be almost universally regarded as his masterpiece. It will therefore give a very inadequate impression of Clough's poetic gift. But concentration on Clough's religious poetry can be rewarding because comparatively little critical attention has been given to much of it, so that it is still not too difficult to offer an original contribution to its understanding.

The book is also concerned with the religious thought and writing of Gerard Manley Hopkins, but in a very different way. So much has been written about Hopkins that it is almost impossible to discuss his poetry, and much of his prose, without merely repeating what has already been well said by many a scholar and critic. The only original contribution this book can hope to make to Hopkins scholarship is to bring some aspects of his work into sharp relief by contrasting them with the corresponding aspect of Clough's work.

A comparison between Clough and Hopkins may seem at first sight a strange undertaking. I hope that by the end of the book the reader will be convinced that there are many lines of connection and analogy between the two poets, very different though they are in many respects. Here, at the outset, I will merely explain why I was drawn, some years ago, to begin to study the two side by side.

Clough and Hopkins are, in my view, the two most significant religious poets writing in English in the nineteenth century. This, by itself, would not provide a justification for a joint study. What challenges comparison between them is the way in which their lives, initially parallel, diverge in opposite directions. Both of them came from middle-class Anglican families; both were educated in the same disciplines in the same institution, Balliol College in Oxford University. Though Clough was the elder by a generation, they shared a number of common friends and were influenced by several of the same people. During their time in Oxford they both underwent a religious development, but in opposite senses: Clough moved from Anglicanism towards Unitarianism and eventually agnosticism, while Hopkins moved from Anglicanism to Catholicism and found his abiding vocation as a Jesuit. It must be a matter of interest, therefore, to see how from common premises such different conclusions are reached.

I am by profession a philosopher, not a literary critic. I approach these poets, therefore, from a philosophical standpoint and put to their texts the questions which a philosopher, rather than a littérateur, would put to them. I do so unashamedly, since each of the poets not only was trained in philosophy but made very explicit connections between philosophical thought and poetical creation.

The book begins by setting down, as a framework for the ensuing discussion, the basic details of the biographies of the two poets. The course it then follows is dictated rather by the chronology of Clough's life than by that of Hopkins. Thus, in Chapters 2 and 3 I consider the early poems of Clough in comparison with similar poems of Hopkins's mature and final years. Chapter 4 compares the spiritual development of the two poets: Clough's move from Anglicanism to agnosticism, and Hopkins's conversion to the Church of Rome. Chapters 5 to 9 compare the thought of the two poets on topics which exercised them both: prayer, scripture, original sin, the sacramental system, and the relation between religion and politics. In Chapters 10 to 13 I consider Clough's major religious poem, *Dipsychus*, a long and remarkable verse drama which has no real point of comparison in the work of Hopkins. In an epilogue I return to the comparison between the two poets and venture the value judgement that, though Hopkins is undeniably superior as a craftsman of verse and as an observer of nature, Clough can claim equal honour as a religious poet.

Balliol, October 1987

CHRONOLOGY

A comparison between the main events in the lives of Clough and
Hopkins.

Clough	aet.	date	Hopkins	aet.	date
Birth	0	1819	Birth	0	1844
Enters Balliol	18	1837	Enters Balliol	19	1863
Fellow of Oriel	23	1842	Becomes a Jesuit	24	1868
Resigns	29	1848	Begins Theology	30	1874
Publishes *Bothie*	29	1848	Writes *Deutschland*	32	1876
Writes *Amours*	30	1849	Nature sonnets	33	1877
University Hall	30	1849	Ordained priest	33	1877
American trip	33	1852	Writes *Eurydice*	33	1878
Marries	34	1853	Begins ministry	34	1878
Examiner in London	34	1853	Professor in Dublin	40	1884
Dies in Florence	42	1861	Dies in Dublin	45	1889

ABBREVIATIONS

C   *The Correspondence of Arthur Hugh Clough*, edited by F. L. Mulhauser, Oxford, at the Clarendon Press, 1957. (There are two volumes, but a single page numeration runs through both.)

J   *The Journals and Papers of Gerard Manley Hopkins*, edited by Humphry House and Graham Storey, London, Oxford University Press, 1959.

L, I   *The Letters of Gerard Manley Hopkins to Robert Bridges*, edited by Claude Colleer Abbott, London, Oxford University Press, 1935.

L, II   *The Correspondence of Gerard Manley Hopkins and Richard Watson Dixon*, edited by Claude Colleer Abbott, London, Oxford University Press, 1935.

L, III   *Further Letters of Gerard Manley Hopkins, including his correspondence with Coventry Patmore*, edited by Claude Colleer Abbott, second edition, revised and enlarged, London, Oxford University Press, 1956.

O   *The Oxford Authors: Gerard Manley Hopkins*, edited by Catherine Phillips, Oxford University Press, 1986.

P   *The Poems of Arthur Hugh Clough*, second edition, edited by F. L. Mulhauser, Oxford, at the Clarendon Press, 1974.

PPR   *The Poems and Prose Remains of Arthur Hugh Clough*, edited by his Wife, in two volumes, London, Macmillan & Co., 1869.

S   *The Sermons and Devotional Writings of Gerard Manley Hopkins*, edited by Christopher Devlin, SJ, London, Oxford University Press, 1959.

1

LIVES OF TWO POETS

Arthur Hugh Clough was the second son of James Butler Clough, a Liverpool cotton merchant of Welsh extraction, and of Anne Perfect, the strict and pious daughter of a Yorkshire banker. He was born on New Year's Day in 1819, and was just five months older than Queen Victoria. When Arthur was four years old, the Cloughs migrated to Charleston, South Carolina, so that James could preside over the American export side of the business. The family remained in America for thirteen years, but Arthur and his elder brother received their schooling in England.

Both boys entered Rugby in 1829. The new headmaster there was Dr Thomas Arnold, the reformer who more than any other man set the ideal for the nineteenth-century public school in England. He strove to establish a tone of moral earnestness, and insisted on the serious study of classics, mathematics, modern history, and science. He encouraged competitive sport in order to promote physical fitness, courage, and endurance. The schooling was set in the firmly religious context of a traditional Christianity which set before the boys the example of Christ and encouraged a life of obedience to God expressed in service to one's neighbour. Little emphasis was laid on the ritual and dogmatic aspect of the Christian tradition, much on critical self-examination and strict cultivation of conscience. The regime was austere and the discipline strict; but there was less arbitrary beating than elsewhere, and the senior pupils were encouraged to take their part in the enforcement of the school ethos.

Clough entered fully into Arnold's programme; he worked hard in class, and performed brilliantly. Despite a frail constitution which hampered him throughout his short life, he achieved renown as a runner, a swimmer, and a Rugby player. Though many of his school writings sound priggish to twentieth-century ears, he was popular with his schoolfellows, and was often consulted by the headmaster. He edited the *Rugby Magazine*, and in his senior years he played a significant part in student self-government.

Having no home in England, Clough had to spend vacations with uncles and cousins. He was frequently entertained in the Arnolds' private quarters at school and at their vacation residence in the Lake District. He looked up to them as second parents, and formed friendships which were to last a lifetime with their sons Thomas and Matthew. His devotion to Arnold refined an already sensitive conscience, and reinforced the sense of duty inculcated by his mother. At Rugby, and during his early days at Oxford, Clough regarded Arnold's influence as a great blessing. Later in life he was not so sure. In the prose epilogue to his dramatic poem *Dipsychus* there occurs the following passage – placed, significantly, in the mouth of the poet's uncle:

> Consciences are often much too tender in your generation – schoolboys' consciences, too! As my old friend the Canon says of the Westminster students, 'They're all so pious.' It's all Arnold's doing; he spoilt the public schools. . . . What is the true purpose of education? Simply to make plain to the young understanding the laws of the life they will have to enter. For example – that lying won't do, thieving still less; that idleness will get punished; that if they are cowards, the whole world will be against them; that if they will have their own way, they must fight for it. Etc., etc. As for the conscience, mamma, I take it – such as mammas are now-a-days at any rate – has probably set that a-going fast enough already.
>
> (P: 292–3)

The trouble with Arnold, according to uncle Clough, was that 'he used to attack offences, not as offences – the right view – against discipline, but as sin, heinous guilt. Why didn't he flog them and hold his tongue? Flog them he did, but why preach?'

Having won every prize that Rugby had to give, Clough went on to gain, in November 1836, a scholarship to Balliol College, Oxford. He went into residence the following October. He was to remain in Oxford for eleven years, first at Balliol and later at Oriel. Both those who had taught him at Rugby and the dons who welcomed him at Oxford expected great things from him.

Clough arrived in Oxford at a period of academic and religious excitement. The reforms of the first decades of the nineteenth century had raised academic standards throughout the university, and the two colleges with which Clough was to be associated, Balliol and Oriel, prided themselves on the devotion of their tutors and the excellence of their scholars. The earnest pursuit of college honours and university prizes was accompanied in many students by a new depth and solemnity in the observance of religion.

Three main currents of religious thought were powerful in the Oxford of 1837 and were influential in the life of the young Clough. The evangelical tradition which Clough had already encountered through his mother laid stress on interior religious sentiment, the sense of sin, and the experience of conversion. The liberal tradition of Rugby saw morality in conduct and motive as the essence of Christianity; it was not deeply concerned with the dogmatic formulation of religious truth. The new but growing Tractarian movement, centred in Oxford and led by John Keble, John Henry Newman, and Edward Bouverie Pusey, fostered within the Church of England a Catholic emphasis on the mystical power of sacramental symbols and the necessity of a priesthood in succession to the Apostles, to give authoritative interpretation of Scripture and ecclesiastical tradition. The movement took its name from the *Tracts for the Times* which from 1833 to 1841 propagated its tenets.

During his time at Balliol, Clough kept a series of diaries which constitute a spiritual autobiography bearing the mark of all three religious traditions. The evangelical sense of sinfulness drove him into relentless daily self-examination, and he kept a tally of tiny sins of speech and thought. This conscience which is so watchful and so critical is in part, as we have seen, the product of the moral training under Arnold at Rugby. But from the moment of Clough's arrival in Oxford the most potent new influence is that of the Tractarians, and especially of Newman, a Fellow of Oriel and Vicar of the University Church of St Mary. Newman challenged the evangelical and liberal assumptions with the claim that Christianity must be sacramental, dogmatic, and Catholic. Clough was fascinated by the charisma of Newman as a preacher, and was disturbed by the intellectual challenge of his lectures and seminars.

More immediate and inescapable than the influence of Newman was that of W. G. Ward. Ward had come to Oxford eight years earlier than Clough; in 1838 he was a Fellow of Balliol and Tutor in Mathematics. Up to this point he had, like Clough, been a follower of Arnold. But when Clough became his pupil he was beginning to feel strongly the attraction of Newmanism, and he eventually preceded Newman into the Roman Catholic Church. Clough was almost swept along with him into Tractarianism and Catholicism.

Ward, obsessively doctrinaire, publicly boisterous, and privately depressive, made preposterous intellectual and emotional demands on his favourite pupil, Clough. Many hours of almost every day he would keep Clough in his room, arguing theology and craving for comfort and affection. Clough tolerated with remarkable patience the possessiveness of his tutor, and shared many of his intellectual and theological concerns, but it is clear that the relationship placed severe strains on his sensitive mind. In particular he found it difficult to reconcile his new enthusiasm for Tractarian ideals with his former submission to the ethos of Arnold, who was bitterly opposed to Tractarianism and had attacked the Tractarians as 'The Oxford Malignants' in 1836.

During his Balliol days, Clough adopted a number of Tractarian practices. Not only did he spend long hours in private devotions and Scriptural meditation; he also took up fasting and other forms of self-castigation. But his constant conviction, expressed in his diaries, of his own deep sinfulness, and his self-rebuke for his lack of sufficient grief for his own sins, owe more to his evangelical antecedents than to his Oxford theological surroundings.

The profound theological introspection of Clough's undergraduate days had a damaging effect, in the short term, on his academic progress, and in the long term helped to undermine his attachment to any of the forms of Christianity between which his tormented soul was torn. In a letter written after Clough's death, Ward wrote:

> What was before all things to have been desired for him was that, during his undergraduate course, he should have given himself up thoroughly to his classical and mathematical studies; that he should have kept up . . . the habits of prayer and Scripture-reading which he brought with him from Rugby, but should have kept himself aloof from plunging prematurely into the theological controversies then so rife at Oxford.
>
> (Ward: 109)

That he did not do so was, of course, due especially to Ward himself; and with hindsight Ward was prepared to say, 'I must count it the great calamity of his life that he was brought into contact with myself.'

Clough's classical and mathematical studies suffered, and although he was universally regarded by his Balliol contemporaries as the most brilliant undergraduate of his generation, he obtained only a second class when he took Final Honour Schools early in 1841. He went to Rugby and announced to Arnold, 'I have failed.' In November of the same year he stood for election for a Balliol fellowship the following November; but on this occasion he was passed over.

In the spring of 1842, however, Clough was elected to a fellowship at Oriel. This was the last election at that college in which Newman took part; and it was one of the final satisfactions of the life of Arnold, who died a few weeks later. Clough remained at Oriel for six years. During this period he became gradually disenchanted with the beliefs and practices of the Church of England. This process will be narrated in detail in a later chapter. One of the most dramatic events in the history of Oriel during Clough's years in the college was the conversion of Newman to the Church of Rome in 1845.

Clough now became interested in social, political and economic questions, speaking frequently on such issues at a private debating club, the Decade, and publishing a number of short occasional articles and pamphlets.

Throughout his years as Tutor at Oriel, Clough formed around himself a brilliant group of younger friends and pupils, including the Arnold brothers Matthew and Thomas. In 1847 Matthew Arnold joined him as a Fellow of Oriel. Memories of the friends' walks in the Oxfordshire and Berkshire countryside were given enduring form in Matthew Arnold's poems *The Scholar Gipsy* and, after Clough's death, *Thyrsis*. During the vacations Clough would take his pupils on reading parties – holidays involving substantial homework – in Wales, the Lake District, Ireland, and Scotland. These were happy and comparatively carefree occasions, whose atmosphere he was later to capture vividly in his own poetry.

While at Oriel, Clough was much influenced by reading Thomas Carlyle, and by conversations with Ralph Waldo Emerson, who visited England in 1847. In 1848 he resigned his tutorship and went abroad to France, where, in company with Emerson, he saw at first hand the Paris of the revolutionary period between the fall of King Louis-Philippe and the election of the future Napoleon III.

In September of the first year, while living with his family in Liverpool, he wrote his first long poem, the one now known as *The Bothie of Tober-na-Vuolich*. More than seventeen hundred hexameters long, the poem was written at astonishing speed, and was published in November 1848. Far from being the theological tract which his Oxford colleagues had expected from him in justification of his decision to resign his Oxford fellowship, it was a lively account of a long vacation reading party, bubbling with cheerful good humour, providing the background for a love story which leads to an antipodean marriage. Religion is barely touched on, but

Clough's social theories are handled, lightly but seriously, in the conversations between the characters; and his egalitarian ideals find expression in the endorsement of the marriage between an Oxford student and the daughter of a Scots blacksmith. The poem was immediately admired by a number of advanced and influential writers, such as Charles Kingsley and William Makepeace Thackeray; by conservatives it was regarded as indecent and profane.

Three months after *The Bothie* there appeared a collection of Clough's earlier verses, written during his Balliol and Oriel days. The poems were published along with poems of his friend Thomas Burbidge under the title *Ambarvalia*. The serious, indeed sombre, tone of many of the poems must quickly have cured any misconception that he was a frivolous writer.

In February 1849 Clough accepted the headship of University Hall, London, a non-sectarian collegiate institution for students attending lectures at University College. His duties commenced there the following October; in the meantime he travelled to Italy. Throughout the spring he was in Rome, where, after the expulsion of Pope Pius IX in 1848, Mazzini had set up a Republic. He was a witness to the siege by the French and the historic defence of the city by Garibaldi. His experiences provided much of the material for his finest long poem, *Amours de Voyage*. This is an epistolary novel in hexameters and elegiacs, which narrates the indecisive love-making of an Oxford student, Claude, who, while making the Grand Tour, is caught up in the turmoil of the siege of Rome. Clough wrote much of the poem in Rome itself during the siege, though he reworked it after his return to England. He did not publish it for nine years, until, in 1858, he placed it in a new American periodical, the *Atlantic Monthly*.

Clough's period at University Hall was not a happy one. He found it no easier to accommodate himself to the principles of the Unitarians and Presbyterians who governed it than to the principles of the Church of England which had troubled him at Oriel. He held simultaneously a professorship of English Language and Literature at University College, and wrote a number of lectures on poets and poetical topics which have survived. But the most productive period of these years was a visit to Venice during which he started his dramatic poem, *Dipsychus*. This poem was never finished, despite several attempts at revision; but even in its unfinished state, it constitutes the most impressive embodiment of Clough's mature religious thought.

At the end of 1851 Clough left University Hall and began to look for a living elsewhere. Finding employment became an urgent necessity when in 1852 he became engaged to Blanche Smith, a cousin of Florence Nightingale, whom he had met in 1850. In October of 1852 he sailed to America, where he spent nine months in a vain search for a suitable job. He was warmly welcomed by Boston literary society, which he described vividly in correspondence with his fiancée. He undertook some private tutoring, and worked on a revision of Dryden's translation of Plutarch. But he found no career which would have enabled him to settle down to married life there. His friends in England found him a post as examiner in the Education Office, and he returned in July 1853 to take up his duties. In June 1854 he was married to Blanche. She was a devoted wife, and bore him three children, but she never succeeded in entering fully into his aesthetic and intellectual concerns.

During his absence in America, Clough had composed a number of short poems, many concerned with the loneliness of the separation from his fiancée. Once married, he found little time for poetry for several years. Any time to spare from his exertions in the Education Office was spent in assisting Florence Nightingale in her campaign to reform military hospitals. 'Little in his life', we are told, 'gave him greater satisfaction than to be her active and trusted friend.' The years 1853–61 were happy, tiring, and poetically unproductive.

By 1861 Clough's health had broken down, and he was given sick-leave for a foreign tour. He went to Greece and Constantinople, and began work on his last long poetical venture, an undistinguished series of tales entitled *Mari Magno*. After a few weeks at home in June 1861 he set off on his final travels, vainly seeking to recover his health. He died in November in Florence, where he is buried in the Protestant cemetery. An edition of his poems was published by his wife in 1862, and a volume of *Poems and Prose Remains* in 1869.

In the year that Arthur Hugh Clough died, Gerard Manley Hopkins was just coming to the end of his schooldays. Externally, neither Clough nor Hopkins lived a life of any great excitement or drama; but Hopkins's life was even less eventful than Clough's, and its story can be told even more concisely.

Hopkins was twenty-five years younger than Clough. He was born in Essex on 28 July 1844, the eldest son of Manley Hopkins, an average-adjuster in marine insurance, and Kate Hopkins, the daughter of a London doctor. The family was artistic and devout:

interested in poetry and music, and favouring a moderate High Anglicanism. The Hopkins family, which when complete included five sons and three daughters, was more prosperous, more settled, and more conventional than the Clough family.

In 1854 Gerard went to Highgate School, where for a time he boarded. Unlike Clough, he was not inspired by his headmaster, and he looked back without affection on his schooldays; but he won a number of school prizes, including one for an elaborate poem on the Escorial. His school career, like Clough's, was crowned with a Balliol award, and he took up residence as an exhibitioner in April 1863.

Hopkins read for the degree in Literae Humaniores, studying classical literature, history, and philosophy under the tuition of Benjamin Jowett, T. H. Green, and Walter Pater of Brasenose. His undergraduate essays, which survive, show precise and original thought, and great individuality of expression. Besides studying the classical texts, Hopkins read very widely in English literature during his Balliol years, and wrote many poems, not only on religious topics but also satirical sketches and items of local Oxford interest. The most important event of his undergraduate years at Balliol was his conversion to Roman Catholicism, which will be described in a later chapter. His religious preoccupations did not interfere with his studies, and unlike Clough he fulfilled the expectations of his tutors by obtaining a first in Mods in 1864 and in Greats in 1867. Hopkins's family was deeply grieved by his conversion to Rome, and his parents were never completely reconciled to it throughout his life. While at Oxford, he made friends with Robert Bridges, the future Poet Laureate. The two grew closer together after leaving the university, and conducted a long correspondence which survives to provide a wealth of information about Hopkins's poetic theories and activities. It was Bridges who transcribed and preserved Hopkins's poems and eventually published them posthumously.

On leaving Oxford, Hopkins took a temporary appointment as a teacher in Newman's Oratory school near Birmingham. He felt drawn to the priesthood, and for a time considered becoming a Benedictine monk; but after a retreat in the Jesuit house at Manresa, Roehampton, in April 1868, he decided to join the Society of Jesus. As a result of this decision he destroyed all the poems he had written, believing that they would interfere with his vocation; he was to write no more poetry for seven years. His last act before becoming a religious was to spend a month in Switzerland walking with an Oxford friend.

In September 1868 Hopkins entered the Jesuit noviciate at Manresa to begin eight years of training for the priesthood and religious life. The novices rose at 5.30 and went to bed at 10.00; they devoted their life to prayer, meditation, learning about the nature of the Jesuit life, and performing the daily household tasks. A fundamental part of the Jesuit training was constituted by the *Spiritual Exercises* of St Ignatius, a thirty-day period of retreat, or solitary self-examination and prayer, designed to fix the novice in his choice of the religious way of life and to launch him on the career of self-discipline necessary for its achievement. The keynote of Jesuit training was the emphasis on self-effacing obedience. The noviciate ended on 8 September 1870, when Hopkins took the three vows of poverty, chastity, and obedience.

Immediately after his noviciate Hopkins went to St Mary's Hall, Stonyhurst, for his course in philosophy. The house was next to the Jesuit public school, but was a separate seminary for the study of logic, mathematics, metaphysics, psychology, and ethics. Hopkins did not enjoy the prescribed texts, but he made an independent study of the theological writings of John Duns Scotus, the thirteenth-century Franciscan scholastic. In the writings of Scotus he saw a theoretical framework for his own poetic attitude to nature. In journals at Stonyhurst, as earlier at Oxford and in Switzerland, Hopkins recorded, in energetic prose, meticulous observations of natural phenomena.

During this period Hopkins's health was poor, and in 1872 he had an operation for piles. After his theology he taught classics to the juniors at Roehampton during the academic year 1873–4: not a demanding task, but one which, according to his own account, he felt he performed badly and painfully. He noted in his diary: 'perhaps my heart has never been so burdened and cast down as this year' (J: 249–50).

In August 1874 Hopkins was sent to St Beuno's, near St Asaph in North Wales, for his theological studies. The four-year course included dogmatic and moral theology, canon law, Church history, Scripture, and Hebrew. Of his own initiative he also began to learn Welsh. He warmed to the Welsh people and loved the beauty of the Clwyd valley. It was while he was at St Beuno's that he returned to the composition of verse and wrote his most famous poem, *The Wreck of the Deutschland*.

The *Deutschland* was a steamer bound from Bremen to America which ran aground near the mouth of the Thames in December 1875. A quarter of its passengers were drowned, among them five German nuns who had been exiled under the anti-Catholic legislation of Bismarck's government. Hopkins was extremely moved by the story, and his Jesuit superior encouraged him to write about it. The resulting poem was a lengthy ode of extreme originality, full of novel experiments in syntax, rhythm, and rhyme. The poem was offered to the Jesuit periodical *The Month*, but was rejected even after Hopkins had agreed to delete his idiosyncratic scansion marks, and it remained unpublished, and unappreciated by the few who read it, throughout his life.

Though Hopkins never allowed himself to care about the publication of his verse, or the achievement of fame as a poet, henceforth he no longer regarded the vocations of poet and religious as incompatible. During his remaining years at St Beuno's he wrote many poems, including some of his best-known nature sonnets, such as *The Starlight Night*, *As Kingfishers catch fire*, *Spring*, *In the Valley of the Elwy*, *The Windhover*, *The Caged Skylark*, and *Hurrahing in Harvest*.

Hopkins was ordained priest at St Beuno's in September 1877. Instead of completing the fourth year of his theological studies, he was sent to teach at a boarding-school in Sheffield; he found the work and the location uncongenial. While there he wrote a second long shipwreck poem, the *Loss of the Eurydice*. He did not complete the academic year but was moved to Stonyhurst in April to coach for the London University external examinations. At this time he began to correspond with Richard Watson Dixon, an Anglican canon, whom he had first met at Highgate. This correspondence is second only to the Bridges correspondence as a source of information about Hopkins's daily concerns and poetic theory.

From 1878 to 1881 Hopkins was stationed as a curate in various Jesuit parishes: for almost a year at St Aloysius in Oxford, for three months in industrial Bedford Leigh near Manchester, for a year and a half at St Francis Xavier's, Liverpool, and for three months in a slum parish in Glasgow. The frequent movements suggest what is confirmed by other evidence, that he was not very successful as a curate; he found it difficult to relate to many of his parishioners, and sometimes found his Jesuit colleagues uncongenial.

From the period of parish work there survive a number of Hopkins's sermons. Sometimes these baffled their hearers, and were objects of suspicion to his superiors; but they were very carefully wrought, and they are rewarding to read. They reveal a strongly conservative theology expressed in a highly original, and sometimes eccentric, manner.

A number of poems written during these years reflect Hopkins's ministry as a parish curate. Thus, *The Candle Indoors*, *The Handsome Heart*, and *The Bugler's First Communion* were written in Oxford, and *Felix Randal* and *Spring and Fall* in Liverpool.

In August 1881 Hopkins began his tertianship. This is a year-long retreat or second noviciate which is obligatory for every Jesuit some years after ordination. He found this a time of peace and content-ment, a welcome relaxation after the depression of the parishes in industrial cities. During his tertianship he wrote: 'my Liverpool and Glasgow experience laid upon my mind a conviction . . . of the misery of the poor in general, of the degradation even of our race, of the hollowness of this century's civilisation' (L, II: 97). Once again, during his tertianship he deliberately abstained·from poetic com-position; he did, however, write an incomplete commentary on St Ignatius's *Spiritual Exercises*.

After the completion of his tertianship Hopkins was never again employed in a parish position; he was assigned, instead, to educa-tional work. For seventeen months at Stonyhurst he again taught classics in preparation for external London degrees; his duties tired him and jaded him, and the best he could find to say was that he did 'not wholly dislike the work'. He did, however, write some poems which bear comparison with his best work, such as *The Leaden Echo and the Golden Echo* and *The Blessed Virgin compared to the Air we Breathe*. During this period Hopkins began the third of his major literary correspondences, that with Coventry Patmore.

In 1884 Hopkins was appointed Professor of Greek and Latin at University College, St Stephen's Green, Dublin, a newly formed institution developed from a small college and housed in the premises of Newman's unsuccessful Catholic University of the 1850s. In Dublin, Hopkins was desperately unhappy. He was cruelly overburdened with the marking of examinations, and he regarded himself as an exile among rebellious and ungovernable Irishmen. Despite his unhappiness he wrote during this time some of his finest poems, such as *Spelt from Sibyl's Leaves*; indeed, the unhappiness itself was the stimulus to some of his most austerely beautiful work, the series of 'Sonnets of Desolation'. He died of typhoid on 8 June 1889. The last of all his poems, written just before his death, laments, with incomparable artistry, the decline of his artistic inspiration. The sonnet, dedicated to his friend Robert Bridges, concludes thus:

> *Sweet fire the sire of muse, my soul needs this;*
> *I want the one rapture of an inspiration.*
> *O then if in my lagging lines you miss*

The roll, the rise, the carol, the creation,
My winter world, that scarcely breathes that bliss
Now, yields you, with some sighs, our explanation.

(O: 184)

Very soon after Hopkins's death Bridges started an edition of his poems, but quickly abandoned the attempt to publish it. It was not until 1918 that he published the first edition of Hopkins's verse, though in the meantime he had included some individual items in collections. Though Bridges did great service in preserving and editing the poems, he failed to appreciate much of Hopkins's genius, and his introduction did little justice to the poems it was introducing. It was not until the 1930s that Hopkins was firmly established in the canon of English poets; since that time his reputation has been unchallenged as one of the greatest of the Victorians.

2

TERRIBLE SONNETS AND BLANK MISGIVINGS

Among the most admired poems of Hopkins are the sonnets of a sequence which he wrote in the years 1885 and 1886 and which have come to be known as the 'Sonnets of Desolation'. They give expression to a sense of estrangement from divine and human friendship, and to an experience of intense mental torment. They were written during Hopkins's tenure of the professorship of Greek at University College, Dublin; most of them were not seen by anyone until they were found after his death.

In Clough's earliest published collection of poems, *Ambarvalia*, there is a sequence of ten poems, mainly sonnets, which bears the title 'Blank Misgivings of a Mind Moving in Worlds not Realised'. In preparing an American edition, Clough headed these poems 'Oxford 1839–41'. On the basis of manuscript evidence it appears that they were written at various times during his years as a student at Balliol, some probably as late as 1842 (see P: 582–6). These poems too express a sense of loneliness, frustration, and internal suffering.

Considered as works of art the two sequences differ greatly in value. Hopkins's sonnets represent his most mature, dense, and finely wrought work; Clough's poems are the work of an apprentice trying out the style of different masters. Clough wrote the 'Blank Misgivings' poems at the same stage of life at which Hopkins wrote *The Half-Way House* and *Elected Silence* and the poems which he burnt on becoming a Jesuit. But there are interesting similarities, as well as significant differences, between the religious sentiments expressed in the two desolation sequences.

Both men write out of an intense religious concern; each addresses an estranged Creator, on the edge of despair, where the only respite is in oblivion. Each suffers from a consciousness of lack of achievement; each feels cut off from the normal sources of comfort in human companionship and natural beauty. Each seeks, by giving form in verse to the blankness of the interior environment, somehow to master and redeem it.

The two sequences were both written at a time of stress arising from uncongenial academic surroundings. Clough found his Balliol undergraduate studies juvenile and repetitive; yet his attempts at university prizes were always unsuccessful, and his second class in Schools was a disappointment to his friends and taken as a failure by himself. Hopkins's letters show that he found his professorial duties tedious, and the marking of examination papers especially burdensome. Both men were in poor health when they wrote these poems. But neither ill health nor the stress of examinations to be written or assessed suffice to explain these depths of depression. The poems, in each case, are concerned above all with mental torment of self by self.

Thus in one sonnet Hopkins exclaims:

> *O the mind, mind has mountains; cliffs of fall*
> *Frightful, sheer, no-man-fathomed. Hold them cheap*
> *May who ne'er hung there.*
>
> (O: 167)

And in another he exhorts himself:

> *My own heart let me more have pity on; let*
> *Me live to my sad self hereafter kind,*
> *Charitable; not live this tormenting mind*
> *With this tormenting mind tormenting yet.*
>
> (O: 170)

His bitter distaste for himself is such that in a third poem of the sequence he can compare himself to the lost souls in hell (O: 166).

The precise reason for Hopkins's self-hatred, and the exact nature of his self-torment, are not made clear in the poems. It is different in the 'Blank Misgivings' sequence; Clough is explicit that his isolation from God and man is the consequence of his own sin. The poems all belong to the period in which Clough firmly believes in God, even though, like many another believer, he finds the belief a struggle. God's continued existence in serenity is indeed his comfort when he thinks of his own sinfulness:

> *Though to the vilest things beneath the moon*
> *For poor Ease' sake I give away my heart,*
> *And for the moment's sympathy let part*
> *My sight and sense of truth, Thy precious boon,*
> *My painful earnings, lost, all lost, as soon,*

Almost, as gained; and though aside I start,
Belie Thee daily, hourly, – still thou art,
Art surely as in heaven the sun at noon:
How much so'er I sin, whate'er I do
Of evil, still the sky above is blue
The stars look down in beauty as before.

(P: 28–9)

There is not in Hopkins any similar expression of personal sinfulness. When, echoing Jeremiah, he makes bold to argue with God, he makes an explicit contrast between himself and the generality of sinful mankind:

Why do sinners' ways prosper? And why must
Disappointment all I endeavour end?
. . . Oh, the sots and thralls of lust
Do in spare hours more thrive than I that spend,
Sir, life upon thy cause.

(O: 183)

Clough's isolation from his friends, like his estrangement from God, is the consequence of his own decision. While Hopkins's lot is cast among strangers because of the decision of his superiors and the incomprehension of his family, Clough makes a conscious choice to leave his friends because they are an occasion of sin for him; he must seek solitude where he can do no harm to others:

Well, well, – Heaven bless you all from day to day!
Forgiveness too, or e'er we part, from each,
As I do give it, so must I beseech:
I owe all much, much more than I can pay;
Therefore it is I go; how could I stay
Where every look commits me to fresh debt,
And to pay little I must borrow yet?
Enough of this already, now away!
With silent woods and hills untenanted
Let me go commune; where my eyes may view
Beauty they cannot hurt lift up my head . . .

(P: 29, 583)

What, in concrete, were the sins whose consciousness led Clough to torment himself? Christians are accustomed to accuse

15

themselves of sins of thought, word, and deed; and Clough's confessional diaries enable us to identify his scruples under each of these heads.

When Clough speaks of 'the vilest things beneath the moon' to which he has given his heart, he is no doubt thinking, among other things, of the deeds of masturbation which he recorded with regular remorse. 'Beneath the moon' captures finely the contrast between the transitoriness of sublunar things and the eternal empyrean existence of God, but it also evokes the nocturnal furtiveness of self-abuse.

When Clough goes on to speak of losing his sight and sense of truth 'for the moment's sympathy' it is social rather than sensual sympathy that he has in mind; the sins are of word rather than deed. In another poem of this period he expresses astonishment that human beings put such effort into refining a witticism or epigram in order to shine in conversation:

> *And can it be, you ask me, that a man*
> *With the strong arm, the cunning faculties,*
> *And keenest forethought gifted, and, within,*
> *Longings unspeakable, the lingering echoes*
> *Responsive to the still-still-calling voice*
> *Of God Most High, should disregard all these*
> *And half-employ all those for such an aim*
> *As the light sympathy of successful wit,*
> *Vain titillation of a moment's praise?*
>
> (P: 26)

It is one of the most constant themes of self-reproach in his diaries that he has exhausted himself by exaggerated attempts at brilliance in party conversation. This leads above all to insincerity: to uttering statements not really believed, professing sentiments not genuinely felt, and making proffers of affection not backed by abiding concern. The frivolity of Oxford undergraduate life is vicious both because full of falsehood in itself and because it provides distraction from the pursuit of eternal truth. Thus he begins the fourth of the 'Blank Misgivings' sequence with the lines:

> *Yes, I have lied, and so must walk my way*
> *Bearing the liar's curse upon my head*
>
> (P: 29)

and in the eighth ('O kind protecting Darkness!') he laments:

> *I*
> *So long, so heedless, with external things*
> *Have played the liar.*

(P: 31)

He was to characterize the different forms of sins of word most savagely in a much later poem, 'Go, foolish thoughts', which contains the stanzas:

> *Go, words of wisdom, words of sense,*
> *   Which, while the heart belied*
> *The tongue still uttered for pretence,*
> *   The inner blank to hide.*
>
> *Go, words of wit, so gay, so light,*
> *   That still were meant express*
> *To soothe the smart of fancied slight*
> *   By fancies of success.*

(P: 308)

During Clough's Oxford years it was sins of thought which oppressed him perhaps more than any. This can be seen in one of the poems of the sequence which is little more than a fragment:

> *Roused by importunate knocks*
> *I rose, I turned the key, and let them in,*
> *First one, anon another, and at length*
> *In troops they came; for how could I, who once*
> *Had let in one, nor looked him in the face,*
> *Show scruples e'er again? So in they came,*
> *A noisy band of revellers, – vain hopes,*
> *Wild fancies, fitful joys; and there they sit*
> *In my heart's holy place, and through the night*
> *Carouse, to leave it when the cold grey dawn*
> *Gleams from the East, to tell me that the time*
> *For watching and for thought bestowed is gone.*

(P: 31)

'Vain hopes,/ Wild fancies, fitful joys' – these took a large place among the sins with which the youthful Clough reproached himself.

There is a recurring theme in the 'Blank Misgivings' sequence which distinguishes it from the Hopkins sonnets: the theme of transition from youth to manhood. It is, of course, this theme which links the poems into a whole and which explains the title given to the sequence. That title is a quotation from a passage in Wordsworth's ode *Intimations of Immortality from Recollections of Early Childhood*, in which he gives thanks

> *for those obstinate questionings*
> *Of sense and outward things*
> *Fallings from us, vanishings;*
> *Blank misgivings of a Creature*
> *Moving about in worlds not realised*
> *High instincts before which our mortal Nature*
> *Did tremble like a guilty Thing surprised . . .*

The influence of Wordsworth's ode is perceptible not only in the theme but in much of the diction of the poems (as, for instance, in the line, 'The stars look down in beauty as before'). But whereas in the ode the intimations of immortality are a source of comfort – tinged though it may be with nostalgia – in the Clough sequence they are predominantly a source of guilt. The ideals of childhood and early youth set a standard which the individual on the threshold of manhood finds impossible to live up to. Clough seeks to come to terms with this not by imagining, with Wordsworth, a world of sinless pre-existence, but by recalling the Christian doctrine of original sin, of human nature corrupt from conception and prone to evil from the earliest moment of individual existence.

This is stated clearly in the sonnet which is the first of the published sequence, but was probably the latest to be composed:

> *Here am I yet, another twelvemonth spent,*
> *One third departed of the mortal span*
> *Carrying the child into the man,*
> *Nothing into reality. Sails rent,*
> *And rudder broken, – reason impotent, –*
> *Affections all unfixed; so forth I fare*
> *On the mid seas unheedingly, so dare*
> *To do and to be done by, well content.*
> *So was it from the first, so is it yet;*
> *Yea, the first kiss that by these lips was set*
> *On any human lips, methinks was sin –*
> *Sin, cowardice, and falsehood; for the will*
> *Into a deed e'en then advanced, wherein*
> *God, unidentified, was thought-of still.*

(P: 28)

No date is given for this poem in any of the published editions, and there is no manuscript evidence which permits it to be assigned to a definite time. But the content suggests that it was written during Clough's twenty-fourth year. The 'mortal span' is no doubt that of seventy years, as described in the ninetieth psalm, 'the days of our years are threescore years and ten'. Clough's twenty-third birthday was on 1 January 1842. It is a striking fact that his election to a fellowship at Oriel was on 31 March 1842; it was this that brought to an end his period of youthful uncertainty at Balliol. In April of that year he was exactly one-third of the way to the biblical terminus of seventy years; he may well have written the poem at that time to set a seal upon his Balliol poems and to state the theme which unified them.

The octet of the poem does indeed suggest a now confident talent, expressing with taut syntax and economic metaphor the moral immaturity and inadequacy which contrasts with the mature aesthetic skill. Though now a man, the poet laments, he remains as volatile and ineffective as a child: he has been unable to realize any worthwhile project. Reason, which should steer him through the voyage of life, has failed to guide him; the affections, the motive force for action, have, because of their instability, proved as useless as torn sails.

We are reminded here of one of Clough's earliest poems, *In a Lecture Room* of 1840. The burden of that poem is the vanity of philosophy, which serves only 'to perplex the head/ And leave the spirit dead'. Philosophy is compared to the broken cisterns which in Jeremiah (2: 13) are contrasted with the divine fountain of living water. Then, in a change of metaphor, Clough asks:

> *Why labour at the dull mechanic oar,*
> *When the fresh breeze is blowing,*
> *And the strong current flowing*
> *Right onward to the Eternal Shore?*

> (P: 24)

Now, two years later, Clough suggests that the breeze of divine inspiration has been no more effective than the mechanic oar of philosophy; it blows in vain on a soul whose sails are too rotten to catch it.

The poet must embark on middle life acting, enduring, and reacting without any overall plan or goal: 'to do and to be done by, well content'. He is not, of course, endorsing this contentment with a life of disordered contingency; the contentment is part of what is

19

lamented. It is a recurring theme in the diaries of this period that he is not only a sinner, but a sinner with a totally inadequate sense of his own sinfulness. Days of happiness are marked down as yet another indication of frivolity to be repented.

The sestet of the poem, unlike the octet, is obscure and unsatisfactory. It is clear that in some way Clough is linking his own immaturity and corruption with the Christian doctrine of original sin, according to which children are born with an inherited tendency to evil which infects them from their earliest days. But in the published version of the poem it is not clear in what form he is giving expression to this doctrine, nor in what way he is relating it to the contrasting Wordsworthian myth of the childish soul trailing clouds of glory from a heavenly pre-existence.

Clough clearly found difficulty in bringing his thought here to adequate expression; the surviving manuscript version of the poem is substantially different from the published one. In the manuscript the sestet reads:

> *So was it from the first, so is it yet:*
> *Yes, the first kiss that by these lips was set*
> *On my mother's was methinks a sin*
> *Nor sin alone but falsehood; for the will*
> *Into a deed e'en then advanced, wherein*
> *God, unacknowledged was remembered still.*

(P: 28, 582)

Here, as elsewhere, one may think that Clough's first thoughts were aesthetically sounder than his afterthoughts; but the content of the verse is not greatly illuminated. Clough's biographer Katherine Chorley has taken the draft version of the sestet as one piece of evidence for her theory that Clough's sense of guilt and impotence arose from a mother-fixation, a desire to return to the womb which manifests itself *inter alia* in his constant use of water imagery (Chorley: 353).

It is interesting to set the Freudian myth of childhood innocence and guilt beside the Christian and the Wordsworthian ones; but it would be anachronistic to believe that we are meant to understand that the deed into which the will advanced was an Oedipal one. Whether one is sceptical or credulous of postulations of the unconscious, the problem remains what, at a conscious level, Clough intended us to understand by the final lines of the poem, in either version.

Why was the first kiss sinful? What was the deed into which the will advanced? In what sense did the poet as a child remember, or think of, God at the time? And if he did, in what way did that contribute to the sinfulness of the kiss?

It is hard to be confident about the answers to these questions, and the ones I shall offer are unlikely to make any reader revise the judgement that the ending of the poem is weak and uncertain. But if I am right, the poem does show that Clough at this time had a consistent and original interpretation of the doctrine of original sin as it concerns childhood.

The sinfulness of the first kiss consisted, I suggest, in precisely what Christian tradition has always seen as the essence of all sin: placing a creature, in one's affections, above the Creator. It does not matter whether the creature, in this case, was the mother or some other human; what matters is that the child, in giving itself to another creature, did not 'acknowledge' God, or 'identify' the creature with the Creator.

Now, most Christians would agree that a child, in loving other humans in babyhood, does not in any way raise its heart to God; but it cannot be blamed for this, it would commonly said, since the child, through no fault of its own, does not yet even have any concept of God at all. For this reason, Christians distinguish between actual sin (sin in deed), which a young child lacks, and original sin (sin in tendency), which it has from birth. But Clough is insisting that the child is guilty of actual sin – there is even then a will which advances into deed. And to counter the allegation that the child does not have the necessary awareness of God to be capable of sinning, Clough calls in aid the doctrine of recollection. The child is already aware of God; or, more correctly, God is 'thought of' and 'remembered still'. It is precisely because God is present to the mind of the child that the child is capable of sin.

The thought is similar to the thought of St Paul when, in the Epistle to the Romans, he discusses the effect of the Mosaic law:

> Is the law sin? God forbid. Nay, I had not known sin, but by law: for I had not known lust, except the law had said, Thou shalt not covet.
>
> But sin, taking occasion by the commandment, wrought in me all manner of concupiscence. For without the law sin was dead.
>
> For I was alive without the law once; but when the commandment came, sin revived.
>
> (Romans 7: 7–9)

21

The role which the law plays for Paul's Jews is the role assigned in Clough's child to the Wordsworthian recollection. Thus the doctrine of the Immortality Ode is harnessed to a particular version of the doctrine of original sin. The myth of the Fall, and the inherited sinfulness which was its consequence, was to fascinate Clough throughout his life, and to inspire poetry of much higher value than this early poem; but it is worthwhile to tease out, as we have done, the starting-point of the evolution of his thought on the topic.

Neither Clough nor Hopkins offer themselves or their readers much comfort after expounding, in these poems, their desolation. Hopkins can do no better than tell himself:

> *Creep,*
> *Wretch, under a comfort serves in a whirlwind: all*
> *Life death does end and each day dies with sleep.*

(O: 167)

But others of the terrible sonnets show that night need not bring sleep nor respite from bitterness.

Clough, too, looks to the night for relief:

> *O kind protecting Darkness! as a child*
> *Flies back to bury in his mother's lap*
> *His shame and his confusion, so to thee,*
> *O Mother Night, come I!*

But even in the night he finds that the glimmering stars, which comfort others, appear frowning to him:

> *As angry claimants or expectants sure*
> *Of that I promised and may not perform.*

(P: 31)

Neither poet can draw, as earlier, upon nature for inspiration. Hopkins, in his Jeremiad, complains to God:

> *See, banks and brakes*
> *Now leaved how thick! laced they are again*
> *With fretty chervil, look, and fresh wind shakes*
> *Them; birds build – but not I build; no, but strain*
> *Time's eunuch*

(O: 183)

Less vividly, but no less forlornly, Clough laments that not only do the 'sweet eyes' of others look and look away from him, leaving him uninspired, but also

> *for me sweet Nature's scenes reveal not*
> *Their charm; sweet Music greets me and I feel not*
>
> (P: 30)

Both poets record occasional shafts of light, glimpses of consolation. God's smile, says Hopkins, 'unforeseen times'

> *– as skies*
> *Between pie mountains – lights a lovely mile.*
>
> (O: 170)

Clough develops the same metaphor of 'lights and hues divine' within a 'region desolate and bare' in the longest and least successful of the 'Blank Misgivings' poems, 'Once more the wonted road I tread' (P: 31).

What, amid this desolation, can the poet do? Hopkins, resolving not to cry, 'I can no more', says:

> *I can;*
> *Can something, hope, wish day come, not choose not to be.*
>
> (O: 168)

Clough, in the final poem of the sequence, 'I have seen higher holier things than these', can only commend the performance of everyday duty:

> *I have seen higher holier things than these*
> *And therefore must to these refuse my heart*
> *Yet I am panting for a little ease;*
> *I'll take, and so depart.*

But the momentary taking of ease may well contribute to dull the ideals which, though unenacted, still remain; and if the heart, even though corrupt, recalls the ideals it will only be with stinging remorse. But even the inner scale of ideals which the sinful soul still looks up to are untrustworthy; the sinner's ideals are no more praiseworthy than his failure to live up to them:

— Hast thou seen higher holier things than these,
And therefore must to these thy heart refuse?
With the true best, alack, how ill agrees
The best that thou wouldst choose!

The Summum Pulchrum *rests in heaven above;*
Do thou, as best thou may'st, thy duty do:
Amid the things allowed thee live and love;
Some day thou shalt it view.

(P: 34)

The chill call of duty finds here an unimpelling expression. In other poems Clough would clothe it in more moving form; but before his Oriel years were over the very notion of duty would come to seem to him a cloak for mindless conformism, as we shall see in Chapter 3.

The 'Blank Misgivings' sequence contains some fine lines, but it is not great poetry. Clough returned to many of the same themes and images later with a surer, defter hand; and the faults of these juvenile works of his are set in relief by the comparison which we have made with the poems of similar mood from Hopkins's mature craftsmanship. But the poems have rarely been given a fair reading. In general, the critical tradition has ignored them, and even those critics who have studied them have shown a strange lack of patience in the attempt to understand them. Thus, for instance, the American critic Walter Houghton, who has done much to revalue other unfairly neglected poems of Clough, singles out for obloquy the fifth poem of the sequence, the first which is not in sonnet form:

How often sit I, poring o'er
My strange, distorted youth,
Seeking in vain, in all my store,
One feeling based on truth;
Amid the maze of petty life
A clue whereby to move,
A spot whereon in toil and strife
To dare to rest and love.
So constant as my heart would be,
So fickle as it must
'Twere well for others as for me
'Twere dry as summer dust.

> *Excitements come, and act and speech*
> *Flow freely forth; – but no,*
> *Nor they, nor ought beside, can reach*
> *The buried world below.*

(P: 30)

The great fault of this poem, according to Houghton, is its lack of precision:

> Why 'strange'? In what sense 'distorted'? How can the heart that is dry for him not be so for others? What exactly are the 'excitements' that come and how are they connected – if they are – with 'act and speech'? The 'ought beside' in line 15 looks like sheer padding to eke out the meter; and because 'reach' (used apparently for the sake of the rhyme) seems to reverse the meaning of 'flow', the final metaphor of a life-giving source is blurred.

(Houghton: 31)

The rhetorical questions can, in fact, be given precise answers. In his own view Clough's youth had indeed been strangely distorted, because instead of being a gradual development towards maturity, confidence, and responsibility, it had reached the point of greatest self-assurance and social adaptation during his middle teens at Rugby; his Balliol years had been a regression in the direction of infantile solitude and ineptness. 'Excitements' in the circle in which Clough lived in Oxford had a definite meaning. John Henry Newman published a sermon in 1836, which Clough read with admiration, entitled 'Religious Worship a Remedy for Excitements'. Excitements, Newman tells us, are the indisposition of the mind:

> Excitements are of two kinds, secular and religious: first let us consider secular excitements. Such is the pursuit of gain, or of power or of distinction. Amusements are excitements; the applause of a crowd, emulations, hopes, risks, quarrels, contests, disappointments, successes.

Religious excitements, on the other hand, are the 'swellings and tumults of the soul' characteristic of the newly converted:

> One never can be sure of a new convert; for, in that elevated state of mind in which he is at first, the affections have much

more sway than the reason or conscience; and unless he takes care, they may hurry him away, just as a wind might do, in a wrong direction. He is balanced on a single point, on the summit of an excited mind, and he may easily fall.

(Newman, III: 336–45)

'Excitements' then, for Clough, will mean undisciplined emotions, whether secular or religious. Like Newman, Clough thinks, and here says, that such emotions are no guarantee of sincerity, of fundamental truth. Nor are act and speech, however freely they may flow ('the flow of speech' is surely a dead metaphor, and as dead does not conflict with the picture of the roots which fail to reach down to the solid earth). But nor is 'ought beside' – one need look no further than the poem itself to see what Clough might here be thinking of; self-examination and introspection (poring over one's life) are no more reliable a guide to the underlying reality than is emotion, speech, or action.

The most grievous of Houghton's failures of understanding is the misreading of the syntax of the fourth quatrain. Clough is not saying that it would be well if the heart that was dry for him were dry for others too. He is saying that his heart is so fickle, despite its desire to be constant, that it would be better for others as well as for himself if it were totally dry and devoid of emotion. It would indeed be hard to find a simpler, or more economic, way to express this bleak thought.

3

THE CALL OF DUTY

The poems of the 'Blank Misgivings' sequence were written while Clough was a believing, indeed devout and unquestioning, Christian. The religious worries of his Balliol years concerned not the basic truth of Christianity, but the question whether the evangelical or the Tractarian version was the more authentic expression of those truths. But during the years at Oriel, from 1842 to 1848, Clough began to entertain doubts about fundamentals of the Christian system, which led eventually to his resignation of his fellowship. The contents of his doubts will be the subject of a later chapter; here I want to consider a series of poems which were, in a sense, by-products of Clough's uncertainty. They are poems which address the question: how is one to live an ordered life when the ideals which should guide one's life are themselves called in question? The poems concern the concept of duty.

The relationship between religious doubt and the demands of duty is well brought out in an article written by David Masson, the editor of *Macmillan's Magazine*, reviewing Clough's collected poems in 1862. Masson recalls the 'standard recipe offered to persons in [Clough's] mental condition' of religious doubt:

> . . . if the doubter will only persevere in the routine of plain and minute duties lying before him, and will abstain as far as he can, during this regimen, from the questionings that have been perplexing him, he will find light unawares breaking in upon him, and will come out of the tunnel at last.
>
> (Thorpe: 144)

The poems that we shall consider make clear that Clough attempted to take this advice with complete seriousness.

The poem which Clough placed first in *Ambarvalia* is one for which he eventually chose the title *The Questioning Spirit*, which it now has in the standard edition of his works. Its first stanza runs thus:

The human spirits saw I on a day
Sitting and looking each a different way;
And hardly tasking, subtly questioning,
Another spirit went around the ring
To each and each: and as he ceased his say,
Each after each, I heard them singly sing,
Some querulously high, some softly, sadly low,
We know not, – what avails to know?
We know not, – wherefore need we know?
This answer gave they still unto his suing,
We know not, let us do as we are doing.

(P: 3)

'The unexamined life is not worth living,' said Socrates in Plato's *Apology*. This poem pursues the question 'But what if the examination yields no positive result?' In the first stanza, the human spirits reject the inquiry of the Socratic questioner, content with a life lived unexamined, whose point they cannot explain.

Why are the questioner and the questioned called 'spirits'? The word was used later by Clough to designate one of the two protagonists in *Dipsychus*, and in due course we shall have to consider its significance there. But it was not often used by him in his early years. As a word for an inner human principle, it is used only five times outside this poem – much less than 'soul', which occurs sixteen times in *Ambarvalia*, or than 'heart', which occurs forty times and is indeed the most common noun of all in the collection. In so far as there is a contrast with 'soul' and 'heart' the spirit would seem to be the part of the human psyche which concerns itself with ideals or ultimate goals. The spirits of this poem, therefore, are allegorical representations of different goals which humans may choose, explicitly or implicitly, to govern their lives.

The poem in its earliest draft began, 'Seven human spirits saw I on a day'. Matthew Arnold, who saw this draft, wrote in a letter of 1847: 'The 7 Spirits poem does well what it attempts to do I think. Tho: I still ask why 7. This is the worst of the allegorical – it instantly involves you in the unnecessary – and the unnecessary is necessarily unpoetical' (Lowry: 60). Clough accordingly changed the text before publication. But there are, in fact, seven spirits, representing seven different forms of life, who speak in turn in the second stanza. In the discussion of the forms of life in Greek ethics, especially in Aristotle's *Nicomachean Ethics* with which Clough was very familiar, the canonical number of lives is three: the life of contemplation, the life of action, and the life of pleasure. No doubt

Clough felt that the varieties of human choice were better provided for by the biblical number seven.

In the second stanza the probing sceptic is answered by the seven spirits in turn:

> *Dost thou not know that these things only seem?*
> *I know not, let me dream my dream.*
> *Are dust and ashes fit to make a treasure?*
> *I know not, let me take my pleasure.*
> *What shall avail the knowledge thou hast sought?*
> *I know not, let me think my thought.*
> *What is the end of strife?*
> *I know not, let me live my life.*
> *How many days or e'er thou meanst to move?*
> *I know not, let me love my love.*
> *Where not things old once new?*
> *I know not, let me do as others do.*
> *And when the rest were over past,*
> *I know not, I will do my duty, said the last.*

If we are to judge by these answers, the seven spirits appear to represent sensibility, sensuality, science, valour, love, tradition, and duty; they are, in a quite natural sense, 'the spirit of sensibility' and so on. Like the ways of life questioned by Socrates in the early dialogues of Plato, they are incapable of giving an account or *logos* of their own nature. None of the spirits can explain the point of the way of life they represent. The most difficult spirit to place is that of 'love', partly because the question to which 'let me love my love' is the response is such an unclear question. In an earlier version the questioning line read, 'Are there not better things above?' Perhaps we are to think of this spirit, at least in the final version, as representing love in the form of dalliance, love as producing oblivion of the world and its claims.

In the third stanza, duty is singled out from the other values for a supreme place.

> *Thy duty do? rejoined the voice,*
> *Ah do it, do it, and rejoice;*
> *But shalt thou then, when all is done,*
> *Enjoy a love, embrace a beauty*
> *Like these, that may be seen and won*
> *In life, whose course will then be run;*
> *Or wilt thou be where there is none?*
> *I know not, I will do my duty.*

At first, the exaltation of duty seems merely to echo the final poem of the 'Blank Misgivings' sequence. But there the call to duty was reinforced by the promise that it would be rewarded by the eventual sight of the *Summum Pulchrum*. Here, the poet is agnostic about immortality and reward after death ('wilt thou be where there is none?' – no truth and beauty comparable to the love and beauty that may be seen and won in this life). The duty exalted here is a selfless duty, which seeks no postponed enjoyment of the goods which are sacrificed to it.

The fourth stanza echoes the first:

> *And taking up the word around, above, below,*
> *Some querulously high, some softly, sadly, low,*
> *We know not, sang they all, nor ever need we know!*
> *We know not, sang they, what avails to know?*
> *Whereat the questioning spirit, some short space*
> *Though unabashed, stood quiet in his place.*
> *But as the echoing chorus died away*
> *And to their dreams the rest returned apace*
> *By the one spirit I saw him kneeling low,*
> *And in a silvery whisper heard him say:*
> *Truly, thou know'st not, and thou need'st not know;*
> *Hope only, hope thou, and believe alway;*
> *I also know not, and I need not know,*
> *Only with questionings pass I to and fro*
> *Perplexing those that sleep, and in their folly*
> *Imbreeding doubt and sceptic melancholy;*
> *Till that, their dreams deserting, they with me*
> *Come all to this true ignorance and thee.*

Though there are echoes of the first stanza, there are also differences. The seven spirits sing now in unison, not singly; all, including the spirit of duty, sing, 'We know not, nor ever need we know'. The questioning spirit himself agrees, 'Thou knowest not, and thou need'st not know' – but he says this *only* to the spirit of duty: that spirit has true ignorance, the others false ignorance.

But what is the mark of true ignorance? It is not simply ignorance acknowledged, for the other spirits too admit they do not know. The goal of the questioning spirit is not merely the Socratic one of turning latent ignorance into patent ignorance. The difference between true and false ignorance seems to be twofold. First, true ignorance is the ignorance of someone doing their duty. Secondly, it is ignorance which leaves room for hope and belief. Doing one's duty without knowing its point is not a maimed form of life in the same way as pursuing pleasure, or science, without knowing the point of the pursuit.

The constant play between 'you know' and 'you need to know' reminds us of Keats's *Ode on a Grecian Urn*. The echo is no doubt deliberate. Indeed, the burden of the poem could be summed thus:

> *Duty is truth, truth duty – that is all*
> *Ye know on earth and all ye need to know.*

Since its first publication the poem has been much admired. It has a number of weaknesses, especially in the middle of the final stanza. 'Some short space' seems padding, and to call the questioning spirit's whisper 'silvery' seems mere prettifying. But its major defect is the emptiness of its final message. 'Hope thou, and believe alway'. Believe what, and hope for what? The poem gives no hint, and has itself rejected some promising answers.

At one time Clough thought of calling the poem 'Through a Glass Darkly' – he wrote this title into a pre-publication copy of *Poems* now in the Bodleian Library (P: 564). With such a title, the poem would appear less agnostic because of the allusion to St Paul's words in I Corinthians 13 ('Now we see through a glass darkly, but then face to face'). This allusion would link the spirit of duty with the charity which 'believeth all things, hopeth all things' and, with faith and hope, abides when knowledge has vanished away.

Clough returned to this passage of the Epistle later. In *Amours de Voyage* the hero, or anti-hero, Claude, says:

> *Not as the Scripture says is, I think, the fact. Ere our death-day*
> *Faith, I think, does pass, and Love; but Knowledge abideth.*
> *Let us seek Knowledge; the rest may come and go as it appears.*
> *Knowledge is hard to seek, and harder yet to adhere to.*
> *Knowledge is painful often; and yet when we know, we are happy.*
> *Seek it, and leave mere Faith and Love to come with the chances.*
> *As for Hope, – tomorrow I hope to be starting for Naples.*

(P: 132)

The hope commended by the questioning spirit may seem empty; that enunciated by Claude is deliberately banal: it is not for any better world but simply for a continuation of the Grand Tour. And when Clough himself reached Naples, as Claude hoped to, he found no comfort in its sinful streets; as he says in *Easter Day*

Of all the creatures under heaven's wide cope
We are most hopeless who had once most hope
We are most wretched that had most believed.

(P: 201)

Here there is no doubt what is the content of the hope and the belief
in question: it is the Christian belief and hope for the Resurrection.
Only, it is rejected as false.

But no matter what the content of the hope and belief that
characterize the true ignorance of the spirit of duty, *The Questioning
Spirit* poses a problem for the student of Clough. For the enthrone-
ment of duty as the supreme guiding value in human life contrasts
startlingly with an earlier poem dating, according to Clough's own
later annotation, from the year 1840, in which he calls in question
the authenticity of the very ideal of duty. The poem is perhaps the
earliest exercise in the vein of vigorous satire which was later to
emerge as one of Clough's most powerful talents. It begins as
follows:

Duty – that's to say complying
With whate'er's expected here;
On your unknown cousin's dying
Straight be ready with the tear;

(P: 27)

and goes on to list the claims of etiquette and usage to be unques-
tioningly complied with – go to church, go to balls, get married,
pay the ready money of affection to whoever draws a bill:

Duty – 'tis to take on trust
What things are good, and right, and just;
And whether indeed they be or be not,
Try not, test not, feel not, see not:
'Tis walk and dance, sit down and rise
By leading, opening ne'er your eyes;
Stunt sturdy limbs that Nature gave,
And be drawn in a Bath chair along to the grave.

The poem is one of the earliest in which Clough experiments
with syntax and metre, often to excellent effect, as in the passage
quoted, where ''Tis walk and dance, sit down and rise' makes the
demands of duty sound like the calls in a children's game, and where
the extra syllables in the final line make vivid the clattering of the

Bath chair on the pavement. But it also has a number of weaknesses, including a choleric incoherent ending.

Despite the poem's faults, Clough was sure enough of its merits, eight years after writing it, to publish it in *Ambarvalia*, where indeed he placed it immediately before the 'Blank Misgivings' sequence. He must therefore have thought of the relation between it and *The Questioning Spirit* as one of dialectical tension rather than incompatibility or supersession.

The dialectic finds its synthesis in the poem *Bethesda, a Sequel*, which was written, perhaps in Rome, in 1849 and first published in 1862. The poem is based on the story in the fifth chapter of St John's Gospel set in the pool in Jerusalem with five porches:

> In these lay a great multitude of impotent folk, of blind, halt, withered, waiting for the movement of the water. For an angel went down at a certain season into the pool, and troubled the water: whosoever then first after the troubling of the water stepped in was made whole of whatsoever disease he had. And a certain man was there, which had an infirmity thirty and eight years. When Jesus saw him lie, and knew that he had been now a long time in that case, he said unto him, Wilt thou be made whole? The impotent man answered him, Sir, I have no man, when the water is troubled, to put me into the pool: but while I am coming, another steppeth down before me. Jesus said unto him, Rise, take up thy bed and walk. And immediately the man was made whole, and took up his bed and walked.

The subtitle *a Sequel* is a clear reference back to *The Questioning Spirit*. We have here an early example of the intertwining of successive poems of which Clough became fond, and of which the most striking example is the later linkage between *Dipsychus* and *Easter Day*.

> *I saw again the spirits on a day*
> *Where on the earth in mournful case they lay;*
> *Five porches were there, and a pool, and round,*
> *Huddling in blankets, strewn upon the ground,*
> *Tied up and bandaged, weary, sore and spent,*
> *The maimed and halt, diseased and impotent.*

Thus the poem begins. Two further stanzas paraphrase the Gospel story up to the point when Jesus enters. But then the story

takes an unexpected turn; the paralytic is identified with the
questioning spirit of the earlier poem:

> And I beheld that on the stony floor
> He too, that spoke of duty once before,
> No otherwise than others here today
> Foredone and sick and sadly muttering lay.
> 'I know not, I will do – what is it I would say?
> What was that word which once sufficed alone for all,
> Which now I seek in vain, and never can recall?
> I know not, I will do the work the world requires
> Asking no reason why, but serving its desires;
> Will do for daily bread, for wealth, respect, good name,
> The business of the day – alas, is that the same?'
> And then, as weary of in vain renewing
> His question, thus his mournful thought pursuing,
> 'I know not, I must do as other men are doing.'

(P: 191)

In writing this stanza Clough was taking sides with the view of
duty expressed in *Duty* against the view expressed in *The Questioning Spirit* – though he takes sides in a mood that is no longer satirical
but elegiac. No longer does he attempt to distinguish between
doing one's duty (as the seventh spirit did) and doing what others
do (as the sixth one did, the spirit of tradition or convention). All
the spirits are now brought down to the most humiliatingly bodily
incarnation; the impotent spirit of duty of *Bethesda* is the antique
equivalent of the duty-bound figure in the Bath chair of *Duty*. Now
only a feeble inarticulate memory makes any distinction between
the call of duty and 'the work the world requires'. The world that
does the requiring is the prayer-book companion of the flesh and the
Devil.

The poem concludes:

> But what the waters of that pool might be,
> Of Lethe were they, or Philosophy;
> And whether he, long waiting, did attain
> Deliverance from the burden of his pain
> There with the rest; or whether, yet before,
> Some more diviner stranger passed the door
> With his small company into that sad place
> And breathing hope into the sick man's face
> Bade him take up his bed, and rise, and go,

What the end were, and whether it were so,
Further than this I saw not, neither know.

(P: 191)

The final stanza suggests three possible ways to remedy the impotence of duty, as a spur to action. The doubts that question the authenticity of duty might be put to sleep, lulled into oblivion. On the other hand, philosophy might, after all, find some basis and justification for duty's call. Best of all, the Gospel allegory might prove true, and some divine motive and sanction provide a spur to dutiful action. But about all these possibilities the poet affirms himself agnostic.

Critics have often drawn attention to Clough's recurring difficulty with final lines. He is often unable to draw a poem to a conclusion which matches the intensity of the lines which prepare for it. But here the dullness of the final lines is deliberate heaviness, hammering home the message of despair.

The appeal to duty, in these poems of Clough's, leads to the blankest of dead ends; and as the poetic talent matures, the vacuity of the concept is exposed with ever bitterer force. What do we find in Hopkins? Is duty ever put forward as a comparable ideal? Is it ever analysed into comparable disintegration?

The notion of duty makes hardly an appearance in Hopkins's poetry. Duty, considered as an ultimate, inappellable value, is indeed alien to the Catholic system of thought. The Catholic ethical synthesis draws on two sources: the Hebrew revelation and the Greek system of values. In Greek, and especially Aristotelian, thought, the overarching concept is that of *eudaimonia* or happiness: the concept of the life that is worth living, *sub specie aeternitatis*. The dominant Hebrew conception is that of the divine law which governs human creatures in every aspect of the behaviour of everyday life. Against this background duty can never be an ultimate value; duty is worth doing only because it contributes to one's eternal happiness, only because it is commanded by the will of God.

This does not mean that duty is unimportant, only that duty is never an ultimate motive. Thus, on the one hand, Hopkins can say, 'A great part of the life to the holiest of men consists in the well performance, the performance, one may say, of ordinary duties.' On the other, he can insist that duty has value only because, as performance of the divine will, it is an expression of love of God. Hopkins's highest praise of duty comes in a sermon on the text 'Thy will be done on earth as it is in heaven':

> [W]ith God gifts will not do or sacrifice, sighs and tears will
> not do nor cries of enthusiasm unless his sovereign will is
> done: obedience is better than sacrifice; seas of tears and
> sighs to fill the firmament are waste of water and loss of
> breath where duty is not done. *Duty is love.* What a shame to
> set duty off against love and bloat ourselves because we act
> from love and so-and-so, our dull neighbour, can but plod
> his round of duty! There is nothing higher than duty in
> creatures or in God: God the Son's love for God the Father is
> duty. Only when I speak thus highly of duty I mean duty
> done because it is duty and not mainly from either hope or
> fear.
>
> (S: 53)

Most commonly, Hopkins makes clear that in Christian thought
duty is only a derivative value. Against the common tradition of
theology, he is willing to allow that God has duties to man as well as
man to God; but these duties are derived from the contract which
God and man have entered into to create a commonweal. God's
kingdom in the earthly paradise, he explained in a Liverpool
sermon (S: 58–9), was a commonwealth in which both God and
man stood to gain, and in which both had duties:

> A commonwealth, we said, was bound together by duty;
> the sovereign was bound by duty as the subject. Here then
> what was the duty God undertook? Providence. That was
> the part, function, office in duty in that commonwealth
> God took upon himself, first to forsee both his and man's
> joint and common good, then by his policy and legislation
> to bring it to pass; to make the laws, allot the posts and
> duties, find ways and means, lend sanction and authority.
> And man's duty was to obey the laws the sovereign made,
> fill the posts, use the means, and put the policy in execution.
> These were the duties.
>
> (S: 59–60)

'Now to duty', Hopkins goes on, 'answers reward or recompense.'
He is unusual among Catholic theologians in assigning duties to
God; he is traditional in seeing duty as a derivative, rather than an
absolute value. The duties even of God are derivative from the goal
of his eternal glory. Neither for God nor for man can 'it is your
duty' be a final motive, needing no further justification.

Clough, we have seen, emphasized the notion of duty partly

because he, like many others in his condition, was advised that if he attended to his duties his doubts would disappear. Hopkins, like Clough's advisers, believed that there was a close, if subterranean, link between dutiful behaviour and correct belief. To his unbelieving friend Bridges he wrote:

> You understand of course that I desire to see you a Catholic, or, if not that, a Christian, or, if not that, at least a believer in the true God (for you told me something of your views about the deity, which were not as they should be). Now you no doubt take for granted that your already being or ever coming to be any of these things turns on the working of your own mind, influenced or uninfluenced by the minds or reasonings of others as the case may be, and on that only. You might on reflection expect me to suggest that it also might and ought to turn on something further, in fact on prayer, and that suggestion I believe I did once make. Still, under the circumstances it is one which it is not altogether consistent to make or adopt. But I have another counsel open to no objection and yet I think it will be unexpected. I lay great stress on it. It is to give alms. It may be either in money or in other shapes, the objects for which, without knowledge of several hospitals, can never be wanting. I daresay indeed you do give alms, still I should say give more: I should be bold to say, give up to the point of sensible inconvenience.
>
> (L, I: 60)

The advice was misunderstood and resented by Bridges. It would not, in this form, have been rejected by the unbelieving Clough. Indeed, he devoted a great part of his life to carrying it out.

4

SPIRITUAL JOURNEYS

In *The Wreck of the Deutschland*, Hopkins makes a contrast between the conversion of St Paul and the conversion of St Augustine. Urging God to forge his will in humankind, he prays:

> *Whether at once, as once at a crash Paul,*
> *Or as Austin, a lingering-out sweet skill,*
> *Make mercy in all of us, out of us all*
> *Mastery, but be adored, be adored King.*

> (O: 112)

Hopkins's own conversion, which he always afterwards tied to a particular time and place, was a climactic change on the Pauline model. Clough's departure from the Church of England, though it would have been regarded by Hopkins as a perversion rather than a conversion, was very much a lingering-out affair.

Until Clough moved to Oriel there is no reason to think that he was anything other than an orthodox Anglican believer. His religious worries were mainly about the state of his own soul. Secondarily he worried whether the most authentic expression of Christian truth was to be found in the liberal, the evangelical, or the Tractarian school. When he was elected to Oriel his clerical uncle Alfred Clough, writing to the provost of the college, Edward Hawkins, could say:

> [Y]ou could not have introduced into your Society a more amiable young man. During his Father's absence in foreign countries I have [watched?] over his earlier years and have never known him guilty even of a boyish fault.

> (C: 66)

At Oriel, Clough became a colleague of Newman's. Newman had moved far in a Catholic direction since Clough had first fallen under his influence in 1838. In 1841 he had caused a great scandal by publishing a tract, Tract XC, in which he argued that the thirty-nine articles, though opposed to Romish excesses, were compatible with Catholic doctrine. He had now withdrawn to Littlemore in the Oxford suburbs; but Clough's diaries for the years 1842 and 1843 show that the two men had several discussions together, though they give no indication of the topics of their conversation. Altogether, the diaries of these years are terse and factual, with little of the detailed introspection of the Balliol diaries.

From time to time there are the familiar expressions of self-censure, but now in a somewhat cryptic form. 'I seem to know nothing except that I am wholly wrong within,' he wrote, within a week of his election to Oriel; and he exhorted himself to humility, self-mistrust, and above all avoidance of 'positiveness' – presumably dogmatism in the expression of his opinions.

If, in his first years at Oriel, Clough was suffering perplexity about Christian doctrines, the diaries give no indication of the nature of any such perplexity. At the end of his first term there he wrote:

> My evident tendency just now is to set up some protection, to build up hurriedly a new self upon hypotheses. Indeed it seems to be already done – & if it were to be taken from under me I should be left with nothing – & so it is clear enough I shall stick to it.

There is no indication what is the nature of the 'hypotheses'. But he goes on to rebuke himself for acts and feelings 'against or without truth', in particular for 'the reading poetry, especially Goethe', in whose *Faust* he had been immersed. He ends: 'Work – Work – Work – Not to be positive – Stat Veritas.'

The Oriel diaries of 1842–3 peter out in a series of teasingly cryptic remarks:

> Not being able to get on without a heart I have as it were chosen my Rugby heart – when I might have better fallen back on my home heart – or might I not have found some rest of the kind with a more round choosing faculty at Oxford? . . . That I have no knowledge of truth to guide my choices; and an excitation making it quite necessary for me to make some choice.

The most important choice facing Clough at this time was that of his future career. If he was to stay in Oxford and accept a tutorship, he must proceed to his MA; and to do so he must subscribe to the thirty-nine articles still imposed by the university as a test of Anglican orthodoxy. The first clear indication of discomfort with the limits imposed with the Church of England is contained in a letter to his schoolfriend J. P. Gell, then in Van Diemen's Land (Tasmania), at the end of the long vacation of 1843.

Gell had exhorted Clough to avoid the religious formalism of Tractarians such as Pusey. Clough replied:

> I do not think I am particularly inclined to become a Puseyite, though it is very possible that my Puseyitic position may be preventing my becoming anything else; and I am ruminating, in the hope of avoiding these terrible alternatives, a precipitate flight from Oxford – that is, as soon as my Exhibition expires, for I cannot think of sacrificing £60 on any consideration. Also I have a very large amount of objection or rather repugnance to sign 'ex animo' the 39 articles, which it would be singular and unnatural not to do if I staid in Oxford, as without one's MA degree one of course stands quite still, and has no resource for employment except private pupils, and private reading. It is not so much from any definite objection to this or that point as general dislike to Subscription and strong feeling of its being . . . a bondage, and a very heavy one, and one that may cramp one and cripple one for life.
>
> (C: 124)

Gell wrote back to encourage him to sign, conceding that the articles were unnecessarily burdensome for the present age, but hoping that they might be revised so as to 'leave a bond, but one as worthy of free agents as the XXXIX Articles were when first produced'. Correspondence between England and the Antipodes was so slow that, by the time Clough replied in turn, it was nine months later, and his doubts had, for the time, receded:

> I did . . . sign [the articles], though reluctantly enough, and I am not quite sure whether or not in a justifiable sense. However I have for the present laid by that perplexity, though it may perhaps recur sometime or other.
>
> (C: 128)

In a subsequent letter in November of the same year, 1844, he explained that his scruples about the articles should not be put off for long. He justified his temporary suspension of inquiry in a manner which is as puzzling as it is unsatisfactory:

> My own justification to myself for doing as I am doing is I fear one which would be as little approved of by you as my objections on the other hand. However, it is simply that I can feel faith in what is being carried on by my generation and that I am content to be an operative – to dress intellectual leather, cut it out to pattern and stitch it and cobble it into boots and shoes for the benefit of the work which is being guided by wiser heads. But this almost cuts me out of having any religion whatever. If I begin to think about God, there [arise] a thousand questions, and whether the 39 Articles answer them at all or whether I should not answer them in the most diametrically opposite purport is a matter of great doubt. If I am to study the questions, I have no right to put my name to the answers beforehand, nor to join in the acts of a body and be to practical purpose one of a body who accept these answers of which I propose to examine the validity. I will *not* assert that one has no *right* to do this; but it seems to me to destroy one's sense of perfect freedom of inquiry in a great degree, and I further incline to hold that enquiries are best carried on by turning speculation into practice, and my speculations no doubt in their earlier stages would result in practice considerably at variance with 39 articles.

He speculates that he might find the irreligious London University a safer environment than Oxford. In London he might resemble the seraph Abdiel in *Paradise Lost* ('Among the faithless, faithful only he'); in Oxford 'what religion I have I cannot distinguish from the amalgamations it is liable to'. He continues:

> Without the least denying Christianity, I feel little that I can call its power. Believing myself to be in my unconscious creed in some shape or other an adherent to its doctrines I keep within its pale: still whether the Spirit of the Age, whose lacquey [sic] and flunkey I submit to be, will prove to be this kind or that kind I can't the least say. Sometimes I have doubts whether it won't turn out to be no Xianity at all. Also it is a more frequent question with me whether the Master whom I work under and am content to work under is not carrying out his operations himself elsewhere, while I

am as it were obeying the directions of a bungling journeyman no better than myself.

(C: 141)

The letter continues with a mannered Carlylese disquisition on the
status of flunkeydom. In describing himself as a flunkey of the spirit
of the age, is Clough expressing blind allegiance to the *Zeitgeist*?
That, surely, would be a more rash and pathetic abnegation of free
personal inquiry than subscription to Christian formulae. Or is he,
on the contrary, lamenting the intellectually servile role which his
present position enforces? Again, is the Master whom Clough
works under Jesus, or God, on the one hand; or is he a personifi-
cation of the thoughts of the wiser heads of the generation? Who is
the bungling journeyman? Is it the university and college dignitaries
who have authority over Clough, or is it those writers and thinkers
whom he is inclined to revere as leaders of the intellectual work of
the generation? Nothing in the context enables one to answer these
questions with certainty. Suppose that it turns out that Christianity
and the spirit of the age are incompatible with each other: which
side will Clough take? Perhaps his whole point is to say that this is a
question which he cannot now answer, and which he refuses even
to consider until forced to do so.

However that may be, Clough was soon forced to think once
more about the constraints exercised by the thirty-nine articles. The
precipitating cause was the controversy which brought to an end
the Oxford career of W. G. Ward. Since the days in which the two
men had been close friends at Balliol, Ward had continued to
develop his thought in a Romeward direction. In June 1844 he had
published a work entitled *The Ideal of a Christian Church considered in
comparison with existing practice*. The argument of the book was that
the Church of England, in moral discipline and saintliness, fell far
short of the Christian ideal. The way to reform it was to bring it
closer to the principles and doctrines of the Church of Rome and to
renounce the schismatic errors of the sixteenth-century Reformers.

The work caused an immediate scandal. In October, Gladstone
attacked it in the *Quarterly Review*; in December the university
authorities announced three propositions to be put to convocation
in the following February: the first stating six passages from the
book to be inconsistent with the articles and with Ward's good faith
in signing them; the second depriving him of his degrees; and the
third proposing a general test by which the articles for the future
must be accepted in the sense in which they had been originally
uttered, and in which the university imposed them.

When the propositions were announced, Clough wrote to a friend:

> I shall vote against all three. . . . The matter is clearly judicial and ecclesiastical; the Convocation is not a court of justice, nor an ecclesiastical body. What right have our MA's to say whether statements x, y, z agree or not with the Articles, or say in what sense the University, which imposes the subscription simply as a Church of England body, understands the Articles? If the Church does not settle it, the University has no business to do so.
>
> (C: 143)

Clough protested against the censures to the head of his own college, Provost Hawkins. Hawkins replied that when Ward took his degrees he must have subscribed to the articles in a sense which excluded Romanism; and 'upon the principles of common honesty he is not entitled to any privileges which he gained on the faith of a Subscription which he would now make . . . in an opposite sense'.

When Clough appealed to Ward's right to follow his conscience, Hawkins replied: 'As to the supremacy of Conscience, are you not giving it supremacy *independently* of Reason, Inquiry, etc.? – If you do, it may guide us to anything, and excuse anything' (C: 245).

The proposal for the new test had to be dropped. It was opposed not only by Tractarians but also by liberals, who saw that they too would fall victims to any attempt to enforce the articles in the sense of the sixteenth century. But the other two proposals were carried in convocation on 13 February 1845. The passages from *The Ideal of a Christian Church* were condemned, and Ward was degraded from his degrees. A third proposal, to condemn Tract XC and thus associate Newman with the degradation of Ward, was vetoed by the proctors.

Ward had already resigned his Balliol tutorship because of the outrage over his book; he now resigned his fellowship too, for a different and astonishing reason: he was engaged to be married. Many thought it was hypocritical for a priest who had written so strongly in favour of clerical celibacy to choose matrimony himself. But Clough in a letter to Gell defended his old friend:

> [A]ssuredly though he violently condemns the English Church for putting the married and unmarried states on an equality, he never said that even a large number of men

were called to the latter, or would do otherwise than wrong in seeking it. The charge of humbug I reject.

(C: 147)

After leaving Balliol for Oriel, Clough had continued to see Ward from time to time. On 11 February 1843 he had recorded in his diary the resolution 'not to talk to Ward'; but this, like most resolutions in the diary, was broken before too long.

The news of Ward's marriage must have been a welcome signal to Clough of the ending of his old tutor's emotional demands. But the demoralization of the Tractarian movement must have played its part in destroying any last vestiges of attraction it may have had for him. He wrote to Gell the following September:

The news to be afforded you is not very important – unless it be news to you that Ward at last has gone over to Rome, wife and all. . . . Newman, it is said, will not go over finally till Xmas but his intention to do so then is definitely announced. It is thought that his immediate followers will not be many. . . . But a great many will be rendered uneasy by his departure.

(C: 153)

Newman was, in fact, received into the Roman Catholic Church in October.

The two colleagues who had been the most famous exponents of the permissibility of subscribing to the articles in a loose sense had now left Oxford and the Church of England. This must have made Clough reflect once more on his own ambiguous position.

In November he learned of a proposal to set up in Ireland a group of non-sectarian colleges. He asked to be considered for a professorship, naming Hawkins among his referees. Hawkins summoned him and asked him what was his opinion of the Church of England, and whether he had any intention of taking orders. Clough responded:

It is quite possible that I may feel it allowable and desirable for me to take them, 5 years hence. At present it is neither. I cannot profess to have wholly got rid of certain scruples and questions which I have had occasion to name to you before. And one inducement for seeking duty in Ireland is my conviction that Oxford is not the best place for clearing oneself from such troubles.

(C: 165)

Hawkins did not consider that 'the personal scruples about which we communicated' stood in the way of his writing a reference, but he said: 'I take it for granted that you are a serious member of the Church of England.' Clough did not demur, though two months earlier he had written to Gell that reading the life of Blanco White had momentarily almost persuaded him to turn Unitarian (C: 155).

In his reference Hawkins wrote:

> I appointed him one of the Tutors of this College about three years ago; which I should not have done if I had not believed him to be a well-principled man as well as a good scholar, and especially if I had not had reason to believe that he was untainted with the principles of the Tract party.
>
> (C: 166)

Hawkins, as provost of Oriel, had suffered much from the scruples and shifts of Newman and the other Tractarian tutors. Clough's support of Ward at the time of his degradation may have made him mistake the direction in which Clough was moving. If so, he would soon be disabused.

The scheme for setting up non-denominational colleges was delayed, and Clough's application came to nothing. He continued at Oriel for two further years. But by 1847 he had reached a position which made it impossible for him long to remain part of Oxford as Oxford then defined itself. A letter to his sister in May of that year contains a long postscript which is the clearest statement we have of his religious position between 1845 and his resignation of his Oriel fellowship.

His continuance in Christian belief, he said, had been partly due to the influence of Coleridge. He went on:

> My own feeling certainly does not go along with Coleridge's in attributing any special virtue to the facts of the Gospel History: they have happened and have produced what we know – have transformed the civilization of Greece and Rome, and the barbarism of Gaul and Germany into Christendom. But I cannot feel sure that a man may not have all that is important in Christianity even if he does not so much as know that Jesus of Nazareth existed. And I do not think that doubts respecting the facts related in the Gospels need give us much trouble. Believing that in one way or other the thing is of God, we shall in the end know perhaps in what way and how far it was so. Trust in God's

45

Justice and Love, and belief in his Commands as written in
our Conscience, stand unshaken, though Matthew, Mark,
Luke and John, or even St Paul, were to fall. The thing
which men must work at, will not be critical questions
about the scriptures, but philosophical problems of Grace
and Free Will, and of Redemption as an Idea, not as an
historical event. What is the meaning of 'Atonement by a
crucified Saviour'? How many of the Evangelicals can
answer that?

Clough went on to wonder whether a meaning can be given to the
doctrine of the atonement which will be consistent with God's
justice, that is, with the voice of our conscience. Whether or not that
is so, no contemporary theologian really knows what to make of
the doctrine:

[T]he evangelicals gabble it, as the Papists do their Ave
Mary's – and yet say they know; while Newman falls down
and worships *because* he does not know and knows he does
not know.
   I think others are more right, who say boldly, We don't
understand it, and therefore we *won't* fall down and worship
it. Though there is no occasion for adding 'there *is* nothing
in it' – I should say, Until I know, I will wait: and if I am not
born with the power to discover, I will do what I can, with
what knowledge I have; trust to God's justice; and neither
pretend to know, nor, without knowing, pretend to
embrace: nor yet oppose those who by whatever means are
increasing or trying to increase knowledge.

(C: 182)

Somebody who held the views expressed by Clough in this letter
could clearly not subscribe to the thirty-nine articles. But it was
now four years since he had been obliged to do so, and the
matter seemed academic until Hawkins, in casual conversation in
December 1847, made a disturbing remark. Clough wrote, in
consequence, a day or two later:

You spoke of a Tutor as a Teacher of the 39 Articles. For
such an office I fear I can hardly consider myself qualified. I
can only offer you the ordinary negative acquiescence of
a layman. I do not think the non-natural acceptation consistent with honesty, but I do hold the doctrine, disputed I

know, but not, so far as I know, authoritatively condemned, that the MA subscription is not perspective and
continuous, but only implies your assent at that time,
pledging you thenceforth to nothing.

(C: 191)

Hawkins must have felt that this explanation was as disingenuous as
anything contained in Tract XC. But Clough, having explained
that his current lectures were exclusively classical and mathematical, admitted that his position was perhaps not consistent with a
tutorship, and placed his office in the provost's hands. Where
Clough was concerned, Hawkins was always patient and con-
siderate. In Oriel with four tutors it was not necessary that each
should carry out the duty imposed by the university statute of
teaching the articles, and Clough might therefore be excused.

He conceded that no one pledged himself by subscription to hold
the same opinions for ever: 'But if he seeks an office to which
Subscription is the necessary passport, he is surely pledged to resign
the office if at any time his opinions shall become changed.' In
particular, in the case of a Master of Arts:

> so far as he knows that he could not have been admitted to
> the MA degree, had he held certain opinions, and so far as he
> has obtained privileges by a subscription implying his then
> assent to Articles which now he does not hold, I think a
> person bound not to exercise functions which in his present
> condition he could not obtain.

(C: 193)

Clough sought to avoid Hawkins's conclusion. Just as subscription does not commit a man never to change his mind, he wrote:

> so, I conceive, until he definitely takes a position opposed to
> the teaching of the English Church he is not bound to forgo
> his privileges. How far this allowance should extend I do
> not clearly see, but I feel the less scruple in stretching it,
> inasmuch as I suppose the University to be protected by a
> power vested in the Vice Chancellor to claim at his dis-
> cretion a renewal of subscription from anyone exercising an
> MA's function.

This power the Vice-Chancellor would use if – to take an example
of Hawkins – a Romanist or Unitarian insisted on his right to vote
in university elections.

47

'But what if a Romanist did it secretly?' Hawkins noted in the margin of Clough's letter. That would not make the vote an honest one. He replied in this sense and went on:

> The same remark applies, as it appears to me, to the case of one who has not committed himself by any overt act. So long, indeed, as he has any doubt respecting his change of opinion, I should say he ought to retain his position. I *should by no means wish to hurry anyone into dissent.* But when his mind was decidedly made up, *upon the best evidence he could procure,* then I think he ought not to wait for the VC's inquiry, but act upon his own convictions. It seems a case to be settled rather *in foro conscientiae* than in the Court of the Vice-Chancellor.
>
> (C: 195)

Not just a tutorship, but a fellowship itself, Hawkins continued, implied a willingness to subscribe to the articles: 'we only hold our places in the College as Graduates of the University.' But he hastened to emphasize again that he was not hurrying Clough into resignation – it might be that his scruples concerned points of minor importance.

Clough replied that he objected to subscription in principle, as a restraint on speculation. The points which troubled him were not minor ones:

> But beyond this to examine myself in detail on the 39 articles, and state how far my thoughts on the several subjects had passed the limit of Speculation and begun to be Convictions, would be not merely difficult and distasteful, but absolutely impossible.
>
> (C: 196)

Under these circumstances, he felt he must resign his tutorship, but did not feel called upon to resign his MA.

Hawkins encouraged him to retain the tutorship until the end of the term, on condition that he did not teach anything at variance with the articles or publicly minimize the obligation of subscription. As for the future, Clough should take time and counsel:

> I am very sorry to see whereabouts you stand. I am afraid of unrestrained speculation leading to scepticism – a very unhappy state and one for which God did not design us. In

truth, you were not born for *speculation*. I am not saying a word against full and fair enquiry. But we are sent into this world not so much to speculate as to serve God and serve man. . . .

I do indeed most earnestly desire that you may not pursue speculation so as to omit action, and neglect the fulfilment of your practical duties towards God and man, and working out, through grace, your salvation.

(C: 198)

On the last day of January 1848 Clough wrote to give Tom Arnold news of his resignation of his tutorship:

I feel greatly rejoiced to think that this is my last term of bondage in Egypt, though I shall, I suppose, quit the fleshpots for a wilderness, with small hope of manna, quails, or water from the rock. The Fellowship however lasts for a year after next June: and I don't think the Provost will meddle with my tenure of it, though I have let him know that I have wholly put aside adherence to 39 articles.

To be a hired labourer, he wrote, was honester than being a teacher of the articles.

After resigning his tutorship Clough went to Paris, where not only was he a witness of many of the dramatic events of the 1848 Revolution there, but also – of more significance for his long-term development – he struck up a friendship with R. W. Emerson, dining with him almost daily. On his return to England he followed a course of lectures given by Emerson, which he much admired; he was relieved to discover that 'there is no dogmatism or arbitrariness or positiveness about him' (C: 216).

Emerson later used to tell the story of his farewell to Clough as he sailed back to America from Liverpool on 16 July 1848. Clough said:

'What shall we do without you? Think where we are: Carlyle has led us all out into the desert, and he has left us there.'

Emerson replied by placing his hand on Clough's head, announcing that he was to be 'bishop of all England' and to show the wanderers in the desert the way to the Promised Land.

Whatever – if anything – was meant by this gesture, Emerson's departure left Clough in an exalted state. On the pages of his diary following that on which he noted Emerson's departure on the *Europa* ('Explicit liber Emersonianus') Clough began a meditation on life, work, and death which suggests he believed himself to have had a mystical experience:

> At the last, if one cannot live, one can starve. Wherefore not? Or present oneself it may be some hungry morning to the druggist fresh come to his counter – saying Sir, I have no bread, give me a morsel of prussic acid. – The Lord gave, and the Lord taketh away. Blessed be the name of the Lord.
>
> Truly indeed I believe that Moses & Isaiah and David, Paul & John & their Master, and with these moreover many that shall from the east and the west, Zoroaster [?] it may be and Confutzee & Zeno, Mahomet & the Teacher of Peru spake in old time as they were moved of the Holy Ghost.
>
> Yet spake they or spake they not, irrespective of critics & historians & transcending all private interpretation, a reality I know, I feel, I see there exists, of whom & in whom are all prayers and pieties, & instructions and inspiration of old . . . communicating indirectly it may be thro' them, directly, I know, to me. Think of it I may if I will as the God of Abraham, Isaac and Jacob; the I am of Moses or the demon of Socrates – conceive of it I can if I choose as of a communion and company of the souls of just men made perfect – One thing alone I know – that that which at sundry times in divers manners spake in time past unto the fathers by the Prophets hath in these last days spoken unto me.

Clough's pen sped over the paper, filling it with pseudo-biblical rhetoric, writing and crossing out, rewriting and interpolating:

> To some special want or weakness some special help may respond – a look of a friend, a sight of a great man, a passage of a book may relieve this or that distemper; the presence of her voice & his eye – Emerson's talk, the discourse of Carlyle, a sermon from Arnold may dissipate this disease, heal this sore. But a Presence I acknowledge, I am conscious of a power, whose name is Panacea – whose visits are seldom and I know not where to bespeak them; but who itself is Prescription and Reasoning and of whom though invisible I feel it is about my path and about my bed & spieth out all my ways. . . .
>
> In comparison of this Art is rigid & factitious, Poetry dull, and love carnally voluptuous. . . .
>
> Truly indeed the watched pot never boils. For four long

hours of God's blessed workday morning I am fain to write and cannot. Through the open windows pours the balmy air – nor noise of aristocratic chariots or plebeian drays, nor yelping dogs, no company or fear of company to distract – my existence is one jubilant alone – the sweetest, securest, undisturbedest solitude.

Pages upon pages pour out, bombastic and bathetic by turns, almost as if the diarist himself may have been under the influence of something fresh from the druggist's counter. Clough meditates on the capriciousness of the muse; but, addressing himself as 'Poor Poetaster', he claims his efforts are not in vain:

> [H]as not my own poor pot here boiled at last – even while I reviled it. My morning's investment has brought me its humble profit: some finger, how unskilful soever, has relieved, running over at least a few octaves, the harp's painful silence; and the Muse wheresoever absent herself has sent me compliments and a message by her half-livery prose flunkey.

No exact date is attached to this effusion, and it is hard to know whether we are meant to take it seriously, or treat it as parody. On 15 August 1848 the diary resumes with sober entries about the rent of houses for reading parties, and misprints in an edition of Keats.

Embarrassing though these effervescences may be, Clough was quite right in thinking that his pot had come to the boil. During the late summer and autumn of 1848 he wrote, with astonishing speed, the 1,700 hexameter lines of *The Bothie of Tober-na-Vuolich*. He published it with even more surprising rapidity; between the first conception of the poem and the dispatch of advance copies, no more than four months can have elapsed.

The poem throws little direct light on Clough's religious development. Indeed, the surprising thing about the poem, to one who has read the diary entries which preceded its composition, is its level-headedness. It is written in a buoyant, light-hearted style, often in a gently ironic tone, always with a degree of detachment from the emotions recorded and expressed. The gentle tones of extrovert affectionate mockery which are its keynote could hardly be further from the hypersensitive, inflated, introspection of the entries which we have been reading.

In July, before he began working on *The Bothie*, Clough had already more or less made up his mind, as he wrote to Tom Arnold, to resign his fellowship when the new academic year began, rather than wait for it to run out at the end of 1848–9. In October, when *The Bothie* must have been more or less finished, he wrote formally to Hawkins:

> I am going to ask you to accept my resignation as Fellow. I do not feel my position tenable in any way. I can have nothing whatever to do with a subscription to the xxxix articles – and deeply repent of having ever submitted to one. I cannot consent to receive any further pecuniary benefit in consideration of such conformity.
>
> (C: 219)

Hawkins still counselled delay; while he was honestly seeking the resolution of his difficulties he was not bound to retire. But Clough insisted:

> I believe it will be best for me, if you will allow me to retire in silence.
>   However little I may anticipate any such result I can safely say that my only chance of a recurrence to orthodox conviction or acquiescence will be found in taking the step which I propose to take in the manner in which I wish to take it.
>
> (C: 220)

Clough remained in Oxford a few weeks longer. Three weeks after resigning he wrote to Tom Arnold, with some surprise: 'People don't cut me at all. I dine at some high tables and generally (retaining my gown, for I don't wish to volunteer to cast that off, though of course I don't mind about it) I am treated as a citizen' (C: 223). But a few weeks later he left Oxford for good; he never again dated a letter from there, and I find no record of his ever revisiting it. No doubt from time to time he felt the nostalgia which lurks in the final lines of Newman's account of his conversion in *Apologia pro Vita Sua*: 'I have never seen Oxford since, excepting its spires, as they are seen from the railway' (Newman: 1967, 213).

Hopkins's conversion from Anglicanism to Roman Catholicism was a much swifter, less anguished, process than Clough's gradual abandonment of Anglicanism for the agnosticism of his later years. Whereas Clough, after feeling the influence of Newman, moved away towards agnosticism, Hopkins, who had been tutored by some of the most influential agnostics, moved in the footsteps of

Newman to the Church of Rome. Hopkins, however, had a much shorter journey to travel. From the start he disliked his agnostic tutors. In a letter to his mother in his first few weeks at Balliol he denounced one of them, the philosopher T. H. Green, for voting to fell a beech tree in the quad: '[He] is of a rather offensive style of infidelity, and naturally dislikes the beauties of nature' (L, III: 83).

From early days in Oxford, Hopkins practised a very High form of Anglicanism, making confession of his sins to Liddon and Pusey, and adopting practices of asceticism similar to those recorded by the undergraduate Clough. Already as an Anglican he believed

> the literal truth of our Lord's words by which I learn that the least fragment of the consecrated elements in the Blessed Sacrament of the Altar is the whole Body of Christ born of the Blessed Virgin, before which the whole host of saints and angels as it lies on the altar trembles with adoration. This belief once got is the life of the soul and when I doubted it I should become an atheist the next day.

He seems to have regarded his High Church beliefs as perfectly compatible with the thirty-nine articles, perhaps in the spirit of Tract XC. For he joined some nine hundred other undergraduates in 1863 in signing a petition against the abolition of tests (L, III: 81).

In 1864 Hopkins wrote to a friend, E. H. Coleridge:

> Beware of doing what I once thought I could do, *adopt an enlightened Christianity*. I may say, horrible as it is, *be a credit to religion*. This fatal state of mind leads to infidelity, if consistently and logically developed. The great aid to belief and object to belief is the doctrine of the Real Presence in the Blessed Sacrament of the Altar. Religion without that is sombre, dangerous, illogical, with that it is – not to speak of its grand consistency and certainty – loveable (L, III: 17).

To another friend, Baillie, he wrote in September 1865 about the difference made to one's views of life by the apprehension of Catholic truths, 'beyond all others of course of the Blessed Sacrament of the Altar':

> You will no doubt understand what I mean by saying that the *sordidness* of things, which one is compelled perpetually to feel, is perhaps . . . the most unmixedly painful thing one knows of: and this is (objectively) intensified and (subjectively) destroyed by Catholicism (L, III: 226).

'Catholicism' in these letters refers of course to the principles which were accepted by High Anglicans no less than by Roman Catholics; and in his early days at university Hopkins was happy to describe Oxford as 'the head and fount of Catholicism in England and the heart of our Church'. But in the course of the academic year 1885–6 he came to believe that Catholic principles cohered only if they were taken in conjunction with the claims of teaching authority put forward by the Church of Rome. The doctrine of the real presence, he came to think, was a gross superstition unless guaranteed by infallibility. 'I cannot hold this doctrine', he wrote, 'except as a Tractarian or a Catholic: the Tractarian ground I have seen broken under my feet' (O: 224).

During the period of disenchantment with the Church of England prior to joining the Church of Rome, Hopkins wrote a number of poems which refer in a veiled way to his quest for religious truth. Thus in 'Let me be to thee' the story is told in an elaborate musical metaphor:

> *I have found my music in a common word,*
> *Trying each pleasurable throat that sings*
> *And every praised sequence of sweet things*
> *And know infallibly which I preferred.*
>
> *The authentic cadence was discovered late*
> *Which ends those only strains that I approve,*
> *And other science all gone out of date*
> *And minor sweetnesses scarce made mention of:*
> *I have found the dominant of my range and state –*
> *Love, O my God, to call thee Love and Love.*

(O: 75)

Thirty years earlier Clough had used the musical metaphor to express the fear that the claims of institutional religion might be delusion; but it was the dance, rather than song, which was the theme of his poem. It is difficult to stand still when everyone is dancing around one; I too, says Clough,

> *The music in my heart,*
> *Joyously take my part,*
> *And hand in hand, and heart with heart, with these retreat, advance*
> *And borne on wings of wavy sound*
> *Whirl with these around, around*
> *Who here are living in the living dance.*
> *Why forfeit that fair chance?*

Perhaps some day he may hear more authentic music in his soul:

> *Till that arrive, till thou awake,*
>   *Of these, my soul, thy music make*
>   *And keep amid the throng,*
> *And turn as they shall turn, and bound as they are bounding –*
> *Alas! alas! alas! and what if all along*
>   *The music is not sounding?*
>
> (P: 22)

Newman, in his Anglican days, had compared the Church of England to a half-way house between atheism and Roman Catholicism. Hopkins entitled one of the poems he wrote at this period *The Half-Way House.* The poem is cryptic, but a stanza beginning 'My national old Egyptian reed gave way' clearly indicates his dissatisfaction with the national church. The allusion is to Isaiah 36: 7: 'thou trustest in the staff of this broken reed, on Egypt; whereon if a man lean, it will go into his hand and pierce it'. Anglicanism is a broken reed, then; but we are reminded also of Clough's comparison of his last days in the Church of England as Egyptian servitude.

Hopkins located his conversion to Roman Catholicism at a particular time and place. It was on a day in July 1866 while he was pursuing vacation reading at a farm near Horsham (L, III: 99). That was the scene of the

> *walls, altar and hour and night*
> *The swoon of the heart that the sweep and the hurl of thee trod*
>   *Hard down with a horror of height*

as he recorded in *The Wreck of the Deutschland.* But he continued to receive Communion in the Church of England for a while, and it was not until near the end of August that he took steps to be received into the Roman Church.

Hopkins later insisted that his conversion, though a sudden event, was due to straightforward reasoning and not to any mystical illumination. To his former confessor, Liddon, he wrote:

> You think I lay claim to a personal illumination which dispenses with the need of thought or knowledge on the points at issue. I have never been so unwise as to think of such a claim. There is a distinction to be made: in the sense that every case of taking truth instead of error is an illumination of course I have been illuminated, but I have never

said anything to the effect that a wide subject involving history and theology or any turning point question in it has been thrown into light for me by a supernatural or even unusual access of grace. If you will not think it an irreverent way of speaking, I can hardly believe anyone ever became a Catholic because two and two make four more fully than I have.

(L, III: 31)

What, then, were the reasons that convinced Hopkins that the truth of Catholic doctrine was as plain as simple addition? To his father he summed up the grounds of his conversion as follows:

My conversion is due to the following reasons mainly (I have put them down without order) – (i) simple and strictly drawn arguments partly my own, partly others', (ii) common sense, (iii) reading the Bible, especially the Holy Gospels, where texts like 'Thou art Peter' (the evasions proposed for this alone are enough to make one a Catholic) and the manifest position of St Peter among the Apostles so pursued me that at one time I thought it best to stop thinking of them, (iv) an increasing knowledge of the Catholic system (at first under the form of Tractarianism, later in its genuine place) which only wants to be known in order to be loved – its consolations, its marvellous ideal of holiness, the faith and devotion of its children, its multiplicity, its array of saints and martyrs, its consistency and unity, its glowing prayers, the daring majesty of its claims, etc.

(L, III: 93)

This gives the impression that an important item in his conversion was a consideration of the Papal claim to have inherited an ecclesiastical supremacy from St Peter. A letter to Liddon, a few weeks later, gives a rather different picture. There, it is suggested that the decisive step was a realization of the inconsistency of the Tractarian theory that the Roman, Greek, and Anglican churches were three branches of the one true Church. 'Can the one Church be three Churches at war (two out of the three claiming each to be the whole meanwhile)?' he asked; and he developed this theme at length, ending with another question:

Has then the view that the whole infallible Church is made up of these three Churches, singly fallible but as yet orthodox, been believed by a body of men in the whole Church for more than 20 years?

He concluded that the only claim the Church of England had on his allegiance was a theory of twenty years' prevalence among a minority of its clergy. He added in a postscript: 'The Papal Supremacy on which you lay so much stress I did not of course believe as an Anglican and do of course believe as a Catholic, but it was one of the things I took up in the change of the position and was no element in my decision' (L, III: 34).

These were accounts of his conversion given after his decision to be received into the Roman Church. The earliest document which gives expression to the decision itself is a letter to Newman, at the Birmingham Oratory, announcing that he was anxious to become a Catholic and asking for advice on consequential decisions. His mind was made up, he said, and he was clear as to the sole authority of the Church of Rome: 'but the necessity of becoming a Catholic (although I had long foreseen where the only consistent position would lie) coming upon me suddenly has put me into painful confusion of mind about my immediate duty in my circumstances' (L, III: 22).

Later, in a letter to Bridges, he described this meeting with Newman:

> Dr Newman was most kind, I mean in the very best sense, for his manner is not that of solicitous kindness but genial and almost, so to speak, unserious. And if I may say so, he was so sensible. He asked questions which made it clear for me how to act; I will tell you presently what that is: he made sure I was acting deliberately and wished to hear my arguments; when I had given them and said I cd. see no way out of them, he laughed and said 'Nor can I'; and he told me I must come to the church to accept and believe – as I hope I do.
>
> (L, 1: 5)

Newman counselled Hopkins to be received into the Church at once, but to complete his Oxford course. But when Hopkins broke the news to his family in October they urged him to delay reception for six months until he had taken his degree. He replied that this was impossible; now that he had accepted the authority of the Church of Rome he must obey its prohibition on attending non-Catholic services; so if he delayed entry into the Church he would be cut off from the sacraments.

The Hopkins parents were as convinced of the importance of sacraments as was their son; they rebuked him for giving up the sacraments of the Church of England, which had hitherto been the means of the grace to fulfil his duties:

> Should not your course have been to frequent her altar praying for light, so long as you had not openly left her? When you were without sacramental grace could you be so likely to be rightly guided?
>
> (L, III: 96)

Hopkins rejected the reproach that he was acting hastily:

> If the question which is the Church of Christ? could only be settled by laborious search, a year and ten years and a lifetime are too little, when the vastness of the subject of theology is taken into account.
>
> (L, III: 93)

His parents' reproaches had some force: 'You say years would not be sufficient to go into the question by Study – therefore you will not study at all, but decide without any deliberation. Is not that almost absurd?'

Hopkins's reply to his mother was a bumptious *tu quoque*:

> The subject has had years to bring its points before me, in fact I had long had the premises and had at arm's length kept of the plain conclusion. Surely too if I had not enough grounds to act upon, you cannot think you have much more. Your not being a Catholic is, I suppose, on conviction that the Church of Rome is wrong; my conversion is on conviction that it is *right*; I do not think you can have much examined the question. . . .
>
> Then again I prayed for light before my conversion: to pray for light after I had got it or to consult Anglicans would have been resisting God.

This, of course, was a resounding begging of the question at issue, namely whether his 'conversion' was a genuine illumination or a temptation to wrong. The letter concluded with the announcement that he was to be received into the Church by Newman at Birmingham on the following day.

After his reception Hopkins continued at Balliol (which had just recently decided to allow Catholic undergraduates) and took a first class in Classical Greats in the spring of 1867. In the following autumn he became a master at Newman's Oratory school. But during a retreat the following Easter he became convinced that he had a vocation to the priesthood, and in the following autumn, after a tour through Switzerland, he entered the Jesuit noviciate at Manresa. It was not yet a year since his reception into the Catholic Church. From that moment on he seems never to have entertained any doubt about the truths of either the Catholic faith or his own vocation as a Jesuit.

The contrast between Clough and Hopkins is clear. Clough did not reach a settled state with respect to religious conviction until he left Oriel. From arrival at Balliol as an undergraduate it took Hopkins five years to reach equilibrium; it took Clough ten. Hopkins's friends reproached him with haste; Clough reproached himself with excessive indecision.

Yet there are likenesses, too. Each of the two men had to defend their decision to friends and seniors whom they respected and who disapproved deeply of what they were doing. Each of them protected their convictions by specious argumentation. From this distance of time any reader of the two men's correspondence, whether Catholic, Anglican, or agnostic, cannot help feeling that Hawkins had the better of the argument with Clough, and Hopkins *père* had the better of the argument with Hopkins *fils*.

5

PRAYER, WORK, AND SILENCE

During his years of religious questioning at Oriel one of the topics which occupied Clough's mind was the nature of prayer: its justification and perhaps its very possibility. According to Thomas Arnold, Clough went as far as to entertain the thought that vocal prayer of the normal kind, far from being an obligation, was positively harmful. It was this concern, Arnold relates, which led to the writing of one of Clough's most admired works, the poem *Qui Laborat, Orat*:

> Clough was staying a night in his London lodgings. In the evening before bed-time the conversation had turned on the subject of prayer; and it had been argued that man's life, indeed, ought to be a perpetual prayer breathed upward to the Divinity, but that in view of the danger of unreality and self-delusion with which vocal prayers were beset, it was questionable how far their use was of advantage to the soul. Clough slept ill, and in the morning, before departing, gave his host a sheet of paper containing the noble lines above mentioned.
>
> (P: 574)

The exact date of this event must remain uncertain. Arnold placed it in 1847, but Clough, when dating his poems for Norton, assigned this one to 'Oxford 1845'. On either date it belongs to a period when he was a Fellow at Oriel and would be expected, when resident, to attend chapel services. In the form in which it was published in *Ambarvalia* the poem runs as follows:

> *O only Source of all our light and life,*
> *Whom as our truth, our strength, we see and feel*
> *But whom the hours of mortal moral strife*
> *Alone aright reveal!*

Mine inmost soul, before Thee inly brought,
  Thy presence owns ineffable, divine;   .
Chastised each rebel self-encentred thought,
  My will adoreth Thine.

With eye down-dropt, if then this earthly mind
  Speechless remain, or speechless e'en depart;
Nor seek to see – for what of earthly kind
  Can see Thee as Thou art?

If well-assured 'tis but profanely bold
  In thought's abstractest forms to seem to see,
It dare not dare thee dread communion hold
  In ways unworthy Thee.

O not unowned, Thou shalt unnamed forgive,
  In worldly walks the prayerless heart prepare;
And if in work its life it seem to live,
  Shalt make that work be prayer.

Nor times shall lack, when while the work it plies
  Unsummoned powers the blinding film shall part
And scarce by happy tears made him, the eyes
  In recognition start.

But as thou willest, give or e'en forbear
  The beatific supersensual sight,
So, with Thy blessing blest, that humbler prayer
  Approach Thee morn and night.

(P: 14, 575)

  The poem has appealed to many readers; Tennyson was among
its first admirers (C: 666). It has been applauded by the devout no
less than the sceptic, though one early reviewer wrote tartly: '*Qui
laborat, orat* is a beautiful thought concerning one who has never
been taught to pray, a pernicious falsehood about one who has
rejected the practice. With such a one it will soon by *Qui non orat, nec
laborat*' (Thorpe: 83).
  The poem has subtleties which are worth attention. There is first
the paradox, obvious and surely intentional, that a poem which
appears to deny the propriety of addressing the Godhead in prayer is
itself an explicit second-person address to God. What is the inward
bringing of the inmost soul before God but that 'lifting up of the
mind and heart to God' which is one of the traditional definitions of
prayer? The poet, therefore, is not so much attacking the practice

of vocal prayer as urging the praying soul to be aware of the limitations of human prayer, even at the moment of uttering one.

The first two stanzas, in particular, in their majestic movement, could stand by themselves as a prayer that might be uttered without misgiving by a perfectly orthodox Christian. They would, no doubt, be most congenial to those traditions which have emphasized the inner light rather than the external revelation as the supreme source of our awareness of God. But the solemn rallentando forced by the alliteration of the last two lines of the first stanza makes the beginning of the poem remarkably apt for liturgical recitation.

The second pair of stanzas develop, now in a more radical fashion, the traditional themes of the spirituality and ineffability of God. Because God is spirit, he cannot be seen by human eye, nor pictured by any inner eye of the imagination. Because God is ineffable, his nature cannot be expressed in language, and therefore it cannot be grasped by any human thought however abstract. Thus far many theologians of the most orthodox kind would agree with the sentiment of the poem. But must the conclusion be that the inner eye must be cast down and the inner voice be silenced?

To circumvent the problem of prayer to the ineffable some theologians have developed theories of analogical discourse; some mystics have spoken of forms of communication with God which transcend all kinds of vision and speech, including inner vision and inner speech. Clough does not deny the possibility of a 'beatific supersensual sight', which will heal human blindness and allow recognition of God, but he regards it as impious to ask for it; such a vision must come unsummoned. Not through the pursuit of mysticism, but through the 'worldly walks' of mundane work is the human will to give adoration to the divine will.

Crucial to the understanding of the poem are the last two lines of the central stanza:

> *It dare not dare thee dread communion hold*
> *In ways unworthy Thee.*

(P: 14)

Several editions print 'dare the' instead of 'dare thee', but the poet must surely have intended the latter reading. (No manuscript survives.) It is unclear what 'the dread communion' is, nor how, being dread, the communion would also be unworthy. Surely what makes the manner of communion unworthy is the insouciant presumption to encapsulate divinity. Again, with the reading 'the' the second 'dare' is superfluous – and this in a tautly written poem where every word counts (with the exception of the two 'e'ens' in lines 10 and 25).

With the reading 'thee' the sense is powerful: the soul dare not challenge God, dreadful as He is, to hold communion with it in ways which are unworthy of Him. Formal prayer and sacraments may, for all we know, be unworthy modes of communion; let us therefore do our daily duties and leave it to God to decide what is the worthy mode of communication.

Man must not attempt to name God, as Adam named the animals; for naming is a claiming of power. When God named himself to Moses it was in a manner which was a refusal to give a name. To leave God unnamed, then, is not equivalent to disowning him; on the contrary, it is to refuse to claim an ownership which would be blasphemous.

The premises of the poem are profoundly orthodox; the guiding sentiment too is traditional. 'Orando laborando' was Rugby's school motto; but a closer parallel to the poem's title is the motto of the Benedictine order: 'Laborare est orare'. Yet from the ineffability of God orthodox believers have never drawn the conclusion that it is profane to use words to describe and invoke him. Rather, they have said, with Saint Augustine, 'Vae tacentibus de Te' (woe to those who are silent about Thee).

Clough returned to the topic of prayer, this time in prose, in a review which he published of F. W. Newman's 'The Soul' in 1849. This was written at the height of revulsion from the religious institutions which he had rejected; the new-found liberation gives rise to expressions of revulsion from the past. Clough speaks of himself as a 'new convalescent' who finds it unpleasant to 'talk of his sick-room phenomena, to re-enter the diseased past, and dwell again among the details of pathology and morbid anatomy'. The essay is polemical; but its target, Clough insists, is not religion but 'devotionality' – 'the belief that religion is, or in any way requires, devotionality, is, if not the most noxious, at least the most obstinate form of *ir*religion' (PPR, 1: 299).

'Devotionality' appears to mean any prayerful relationship to God which takes the form of a felt or imagined sense of closeness to a personal individual: 'Is it otherwise than superstitious for a Protestant devotee to recognise the sensuous presence of the Son, or for the Romish to believe in the visits of the Mother, who lived and died in Palestine eighteen centuries ago?' Clough does not absolutely rule out the possibility of some such experiential contact with the divine; but it is unsafe 'to ascribe an objective actual character to any picture of our imagination'.

To believe such spiritual communion possible is perhaps not unwise; to expect it is perilous; to seek it pernicious. To make it our business here is simply suicidal.

(PPR, 1: 299)

In attacking 'devotionality' Clough is alternately splenetic and patronizing:

Be it far from either the present, or any other reviewer, to speak lightly, or otherwise than reverently, of the mysterious instinct of prayer. In no list of gases, mephitic or otherwise, shall this delicate exhalation of man's inmost humanity be written down; let no man desire to analyse and decompose it. The overflowings of the grateful heart, the aspiration of the imprisoned, the cries of the troubled soul, shall not be tried in any chemist's retort or crucible. All that, here at least, shall be said is that, for the spirit's health, it is essential that these effluxes be limited; better far that this precious imponderable lie crystallised or metallized within us, than be disengaged and let free to escape in profuse and idle volumes into the vast uncongenial expanses of atmosphere.

(PPR, 1: 298)

Two forms of devotionality are singled out for attack. There is the extreme form, practised by the Roman Catholic contemplative:

To sit at the feet of an Unseen Visitant, to gaze on a celestial countenance, visible to the entranced one alone, and to listen to words spiritually discerned, inaudible to the carnal, this is the one thing needful with which Martha must not interfere, however much Mary may be needed for the many things of service.

(PPR, 1: 299)

This is a consistent life, though it demands unblest Marthas to provide material support for the beatified Marys.

But most people combine devotionality with the cares and duties of the world, and for them the problem is that the hours spent in devotion provide no real guidance for practical living; they are therefore 'forced to take refuge in a position either of mere fantastical caprice or hard unmeaning formalism'. Perhaps they take every suggestion of the fancy as a prompting of the divine Spirit; perhaps they are reduced to tossing a coin, to 'find the spirit of wisdom in the head or tail of an appointed providential sixpence'.

> Yet indeed be thankful, O ye Protestants, for to you belongs this special ill; rejoice and be triumphant, the dead sixpence is less pernicious than the living confessor.
>
> (PPR, 1: 300)

Clough goes on to mock those who claim to have discovered God as the designer of the universe ('Was it nobody, think you, that put salt in the sea for us?'). The true religion, he insists, is the religion of silence:

> Let there be priests, if you please, to preserve the known, and let them, as is their office, magnify their office, and say, It is all. But there shall also be priests to vindicate the unknown; nor shall it be accounted presumption in them to maintain, – it is not all.
>
> (PPR, 1: 300)

The review is an embarrassing piece of work, full of insensitive gibe and clumsy humour. Much of the thought is the same as that of *Qui Laborat, Orat*, but the tone and touch are very different. The piece is well described by Clough himself, anticipating the reaction of his readers, as 'a penny imitation of the great Carlylian trumpet'. Only in one paragraph does he drop the bullying and bantering tone and recover something of the dignity of his former work:

> We are here, however we came, to do something, to fulfil our *ergon*, to live according to nature, to serve God: the world is here, however it came here, to be made something of by our hands. Not by prayer, but by examination, examination, not of ourselves, but of the world, shall we find out what to do, and how to do it. Not by looking up into our Master's face shall we learn the meaning of the book which he has put into our hands; not by hanging on to our mother's apron strings shall we perform the errand on which she has sent us; not by saying, 'I go, Sir' shall we do work in the vineyard; nor by exclaiming 'Lord, Lord!' enter into the Kingdom of Heaven.
>
> (PPR, 1: 304)

One of the weaknesses of the piece is that Clough does not seem to realize how easily his own solemn passages could be subjected to the deflationary sarcasm he has exercised on the devout. It was only when he came to write *Dipsychus* that he found the way to combine his satiric talent with his liturgical gift in an aesthetically satisfying philosophico-theological dialectic.

Meanwhile, Clough's departure from Oriel had not put an end to practical perplexities about the conduct of prayer and worship. He was a candidate for the principalship of the new semi-collegiate University Hall in London, a non-sectarian establishment set up by Presbyterians and Unitarians 'to maintain the sanctity of private judgment in matters of religion'. He was asked by the interviewing committee whether he would be willing to conduct prayers. He replied:

> I do not feel myself competent to undertake the conduct or superintendence of any prayers: nor can I in any way pledge myself to be present. Any attendance I might give would be that of a private person, in no way official; it would be similar to that of a member of a family at domestic worship; it would be a matter of conformity, not of individual choice; – my own private feeling meantime being much the same as that of the Quakers with whom I imagine prayer is left to spontaneous emotion; so that I confess I should prefer any arrangement which would make my absence not unnatural.
>
> (C: 230)

Despite this disdainful letter, he was given the principalship. Arrangements were made for a divine to conduct the daily service and teach theology.

In Clough's post-Anglican period his most successful attempt to give expression to his sentiments on prayer comes in the poem *Hymnos Aumnos* ('a hymn, yet not a hymn') which he wrote in 1851. The first stanza begins, like *Qui Laborat, Orat*, with an invocation to the incomprehensible Godhead:

> *O Thou whose image in the shrine*
> *Of human spirits dwells divine;*
> *Which from that precinct once conveyed,*
> *To be to outer day displayed,*
> *Doth vanish, part, and leave behind*
> *Mere blank and void of empty mind,*
> *Which wilful fancy seeks in vain*
> *With casual shapes to fill again.*
>
> (P: 311)

Once again the starting-point is the evangelical assumption that the place to look for God is in the individual's inmost soul. Search, so conducted, is bound to fail. Attempts to give public expression to the God encountered in the soul yield only meaningless, self-contradictory utterances ('blank and void') or images unconnected with reality ('casual shapes').

The second stanza develops the theme of the impotence of human utterance to embody the divine. In the third the poet proclaims that silence – inner as well as outer – is the only response to the ineffable:

> *O thou, in that mysterious shrine*
> *Enthroned, as we must say, divine!*
> *I will not frame one thought of what*
> *Thou mayest either be or not.*
> *I will not prate of 'thus' and 'so'*
> *And be profane with 'yes' or 'no'.*
> *Enough that in our soul and heart*
> *Thou, whatso'er thou may'st be, art.*
>
> (P: 311)

The agnosticism is radical; the *via negativa* is rejected as firmly as the *via positiva*. Not only can we not say of God what He is, we are equally impotent to say what He is not. The possibility, therefore, cannot be ruled out that one or other of the revelations claimed by others may after all be true:

> *Unseen, secure in that high shrine*
> *Acknowledged present and divine,*
> *I will not ask some upper air,*
> *Some future day, to place thee there;*
> *Nor say, nor yet deny, such men*
> *Or women saw thee thus and then:*
> *Thy name was such, and there or here*
> *To him or her thou didst appear.*
>
> (P: 312)

'Nor say, nor yet deny' – Clough wishes to make room for the possibility that the 'devotionist' may have the truth after all; and in the next and final stanza he even allows that the devotionist's grip on the truth may deserve the title 'knowledge'. But at the same time in the final stanza he pushes his own agnosticism a stage further.

67

Perhaps there is no way in which God dwells – even ineffably – as an object of the inner vision of the soul. Perhaps we should reconcile ourselves to the idea that God is not to be found at all by human minds. But even that does not take away all possibility of prayer.

> *Do only thou in that dim shrine,*
> *Unknown or known, remain, divine;*
> *There, or if not, at least in eyes*
> *That scan the fact that round them lies.*
> *The hand to sway, the judgment guide,*
> *In sight and sense, thyself divide:*
> *Be thou but there, – in soul and heart,*
> *I will not ask to feel thou art.*

(P: 312)

The soul reconciled to the truth that there can be no analogue of seeing or feeling God, that nothing can be meaningfully said about Him, can yet address Him and pray to be illuminated by His power and be the instrument of His action. But does not this presume that God can after all be described: at least as a powerful agent who can hear our prayers? No, the prayer need not assume the truth of that; only its *possibility* is needed to make prayer for help a rational response to human impotence.

The poem was not published until after Clough's death. But there is reason to think that he remained content with it as an expression of his final position. Two years after writing it, he wrote from America to his future wife:

> I was just looking into a book which I brought with me at what is called there *hymnos aumnos* – have you got it in yours – it wants a good deal of mending as it stands chez moi, but it is on the whole in sense very satisfactory to me still.

(C: 427)

It is clear from his letters that in later life Clough attended church services from time to time, but that he was commonly uncomfortable when doing so. In 1856 he wrote to William Allingham:

> I find myself recoil as yet from any Church or Chapel and even from the family prayers into which circumstances sometimes hurry one. I could almost believe it to be one's duty to take up one's parable and protest, or at any rate to take oneself off. Yet I hesitate – and probably, but for the

pressure of circumambient dogmatism and conformity, should not feel the impulse.

(C, 2: 452)

The contrast between Clough's later years and the later life of Hopkins, it may well seem, could hardly be greater: Clough, irregularly and unhappily attending church out of motives of courtesy; Hopkins, saying Mass daily and reciting the hours of the breviary throughout his life as a Jesuit. Yet, when one looks at what Hopkins wrote about prayer, whether in poetry or in prose, there are some surprising points of contact.

In the Lent of 1866, just before he decided to join the Catholic Church, Hopkins wrote a poem entitled *Nondum*, with an epigraph from Isaiah, 'Verily thou are a God that hidest thyself' (45: 15):

> *God, though to Thee our psalm we raise*
> *No answering voice comes from the skies;*
> *To Thee the trembling sinner prays*
> *But no forgiving voice replies;*
> *Our prayer seems lost in desert ways,*
> *Our hymn in the vast silence dies.*
>
> *We see the glories of the earth*
> *But not the hand that wrought them all:*
> *Night to a myriad worlds gives birth,*
> *Yet like a lighted empty hall*
> *Where stands no host at door or hearth*
> *Vacant creation's lamps appal.*
>
> *We guess; we clothe Thee, unseen King*
> *With attributes we deem are meet;*
> *Each in his own imagining*
> *Sets us a shadow in Thy seat;*
> *Yet know not how our gifts to bring,*
> *Where seek Thee with unsandalled feet.*

(O: 81)

In this third stanza particularly there is a striking similarity with the thoughts expressed in *Qui Laborat, Orat* and in *Hymnos Aumnos*: the inappropriateness of the attributes with which human thought clothes God, the inadequacy of the images which the imagination sets up of God within the shrine of the mind, the ignorance of humans about worthy methods of communion with God. The final four stanzas, too, express sentiments that are familiar to readers of Clough:

And Thou art silent, whilst Thy world
Contends about its many creeds
And hosts confront with flags unfurled
And zeal is flushed and pity bleeds
And truth is heard, with tears impearled,
A moaning voice among the reeds.

My hand upon my lips I lay;
The breast's desponding sob I quell
I move along life's tomb-decked way
And listen to the passing bell
Summoning men from speechless day
To death's more silent, darker spell.

Oh, till Thou givest that sense beyond,
To shew Thee that Thou art, and near,
Let patience with her chastening wand
Dispel the doubt and dry the tear;
And lead me child-like by the hand
If still in darkness, not in fear.

Speak! whisper to my watching heart
One word – as when a mother speak
Soft, when she sees her infant start,
Till dimpled joy steals o'er its cheeks.
Then, to behold Thee as Thou art,
I'll wait till morn eternal breaks.

(O: 82)

'My hand upon my lips I lay' is not too distant from Clough's insistence that in times of darkness the best worship of God may be silence. Clough does not 'ask to feel Thou art', just as Hopkins knows that he cannot yet expect 'that sense beyond/ to shew Thee that thou Art, and near'. Both, in the meantime, pray to be guided – the hand to be swayed, the step to be led. And both are resigned to wait for a final revelation: as Clough, in the poem *The New Sinai*, exhorted the reader faced with the challenge of atheism:

No God, it saith; ah wait in faith
God's self-completing plan;
Receive it not, but leave it not,
And wait it out, O Man!

(P: 17)

Hopkins wrote little about the nature of prayer. In his own life, the liturgical programme prescribed for a Jesuit priest provided the staple, institutional framework of prayer; his private prayer fell into the form of meditation prescribed in the *Spiritual Exercises* of St Ignatius. A Jesuit meditation began with a number of 'preludes' in which the imagination was to be fixed on the concrete, pictorial aspects of the spiritual theme to be considered; thus a meditation on the Nativity would begin with an attempt to render vivid to the imagination the sights, sounds, smells, and feel of the stable of Bethlehem. The main part of the meditation consisted of three 'points' or intellectual considerations of the spiritual significance of the topic of the meditation. Finally, there would be a 'colloquy', a second-person prayer to God the Father or to Jesus, followed by a number of resolutions for practical action. This Ignatian pattern is to be found in Hopkins's published meditations (though the imaginative preludes often spill over into the intellectual 'points', as in his meditation on hell in S: 241), but can also be perceived as providing the framework for some of the major poems such as *The Wreck of the Deutschland*.

The theme of Clough's *Qui Laborat, Orat* was one which was familiar and congenial to Hopkins. The humblest duties of human beings turn into prayer if they are performed for the glory of God:

> It is not only prayer that gives God glory but work. Smiting on an anvil, sawing a beam, whitewashing a wall, driving horses, sweeping, scouring, everything gives God some glory if being in his grace you do it as your duty. To go to communion worthily gives God great glory, but to take food in thankfulness and temperance gives him glory too. To lift up the hands in prayer gives God glory, but a man with a dungfork in his hand, a woman with a sloppail, give him glory too.
>
> (S: 241)

Hopkins would not have agreed with Clough that the most appropriate form of prayer is silence. But he frequently enunciates a parallel principle of abnegation: the safest way to thank God for his gifts is to renounce the enjoyment of them. This doctrine receives its most eloquent enunciation in *The Leaden Echo and the Golden Echo*, designed for Hopkins's drama on St Winifred. The leaden echo in the poem laments that there is no way, no catch or key, to keep beauty from decaying and vanishing. The golden echo answers the call of 'despair' with the call to 'spare'; there is a key to preserve the flower of beauty:

Winning ways, airs innocent, maidenmanners, sweet looks, loose
  locks, long locks, lovelocks, gaygear, going gallant, girlgrace –
Resign them, sign them, seal them, send them, motion them with
  breath,
And with sighs soaring, soaring sighs, deliver
Them; beauty-in-the-ghost, deliver it, early now, long before death
Give beauty back, beauty, beauty, beauty back to God beauty's self
  and beauty's giver.
See; not a hair is, not an eyelash, not the least lash lost; every hair
Is, hair of the head, numbered.

(O: 156)

And how is beauty to be given back to God? Most obviously, by thanking Him for it, and by enjoying it within the bounds of His law; but also, and especially, by the way of sacrifice, by forgoing its enjoyment as a form of self-denial. From time to time we are given clues to this in Hopkins's own life – as when, in recording the natural beauty of the Stonyhurst countryside in spring 1869, Hopkins says:

> The elms have long been in red bloom and yesterday I saw small leaves on the brushwood at their roots. Some primroses out. But a penance which I was doing from Jan. 25 to July 25 prevented my seeing much that half-year.

(J: 121)

Self-denial as sacrifice to God was not something that was ever comprehensible to Clough, whether in his agnostic or his Christian period. As an undergraduate he practised, no less enthusiastically than Hopkins, forms of self-mortification. But the motivation was a different one; it was to bring home, by self-punishment, the heinousness of one's sins. Self-denial was not a form of prayer or sacrifice.

Towards the end of his life, Hopkins found that he could no longer practise the Ignatian form of prayer. In the retreat notes of the final year of his life we read:

> I could lead this life well enough if I had bodily energy and cheerful spirits. However, these God will not give me. The other part, the more important, remains, my inward service.
>
> I was continuing this train of thought this evening when I began to enter on that course of loathing and hopelessness

which I have so often felt before, which made me fear madness and which led me to give up the practice of meditation except, as now in retreat, and here it is again.

(S: 262)

For both the agnostic and the Jesuit, private prayer to God was urgently important and almost impossible; in Clough's case for intellectual reasons, and in Hopkins's for psychological ones. But for both prayer was a matter not so much of choice as of necessity. As Claude put it in *Amours de Voyage*:

[M]en pray, without asking
Whether one really exist to hear or do anything for them,
Simply impelled by the need of the moment to turn to a Being
In the conception of whom there is freedom from all limitation

(P: 128)

6

THE WORD OF THE LORD

As an undergraduate at Balliol, Clough was a devoted student of the Bible. He meditated regularly on the sacred text, and frequently copied into his diaries passages in Greek from the Gospels and Epistles. He treated the Evangelists as serious historians, and devoted effort to harmonizing the different accounts of Jesus' life. From time to time he would reprove himself for having approached the Scriptures in too critical a spirit; for acting the interpreter, rather than reading the New Testament solely with a view to impressing upon himself God's hatred of sin.

An important part in Clough's estrangement from orthodox Christianity was a growing distrust in the historicity of the Gospels, derived, it seems, from the reading of German works of criticism. Thomas Arnold tells us that 'He became acquainted with the writings of the Tubingen School, and seems to have held that the mystical theory of Strauss, and the New Testament chronology of Baur, were alike unanswerable' (*The Nineteenth Century*, January 1898).

Baur attributed the New Testament synthesis to the second century AD, regarding it as a late attempt at reconciliation between Judaism and universalism in primitive Christianity. Strauss rejected all the miraculous and supernatural elements in the Gospels, and regarded the presentation of Christ by the Evangelists as the product of a collective myth. Strauss's *Life of Jesus* was translated into English by George Eliot in 1846.

The anti-supernaturalism of the German critics was based on philosophical rather than strictly historical grounds, and the late dating of the New Testament writings would nowadays be rejected even by the most secular of critics. But Strauss's thought had a powerful influence on Clough, to be seen in both his prose and his poetry.

Hawkins, trying to check Clough's doubts at the time of his departure from Oriel, urged him to study the Evidences of the Christian Revelation. He recommended a wide course of reading of (rather old-fashioned) divines; but he opined that a serious study of the teaching and character of Christ in the four Gospels would convince the doubter of the authenticity of those books and of the fundamental truths of Christianity. He went on:

> I suspect however that many of your difficulties turn upon the O.T. . . . But your faith could scarcely be shaken by subordinate difficulties in the O.T. if it were well established in the Revelation disclosed to us by Christ and His Apostles.
>
> (C: 226)

In dealing with Hawkins, Clough took a protective stance towards his own disbelief, and he was reluctant to state the detailed nature of his doubts. But it woud have been discourteous totally to ignore Hawkins's patient concern, and four months and several letters later he gave a response which sets out some of his problems under guise of reporting on the current 'difficulties of young men'. The Old Testament was not mentioned explicitly, but, with regard to the Evidences, Hawkins was told:

> [T]here is a general feeling that Miracles are poor proofs. The doctrine must prove them, not they the doctrine. Can we be sure that anything is really a miracle? – If not the result of an unknown law of Nature, it may yet be 'a permitted trial' – like bad men's prosperity. – Again, books like Strauss's life of Jesus have disturbed the historical foundations of Christianity.
>
> (C: 249)

Nearly a year earlier, in the letter to his sister quoted in an earlier chapter, Clough had expressed his adherence to Strauss's view that the essence of Christianity could be detached from its historical setting: 'Trust in God's Justice and Love, and belief in his Commands as written in our Conscience, stand unshaken, though Matthew, Mark, Luke and John, or even St Paul, were to fall' (C: 182).

These sentiments were given poetic form in some verses drafted by Clough in an 1847 notebook, but not published until 1869, eight years after his death. The poem is entitled *Epi-Strauss-ion*:

> *Matthew and Mark and Luke and holy John*
> *Evanished all and gone!*
> *Yes, he that erst, his dusky curtains quitting,*
> *Through Eastern pictured panes his level beams transmitting*

With gorgeous portraits blent,
On them his glories intercepted spent,
Southwestering now, through windows plainly glassed,
On the inside face his radiance keen hath cast,
And in the lustre lost, invisible and gone,
Are, say you, Matthew, Mark and Luke and holy John?
Lost, is it? lost, to be recovered never?
However,
The place of worship the meantime with light
Is, if less richly, more sincerely bright,
And in blue skies the Orb is manifest to sight.

(P: 163)

The single controlling image is powerful. The morning sun shines into the church through the stained-glass images of the Evangelists in the chancel windows; the afternoon sun, shining through the plain glass of the nave windows, illuminates the church more brightly but less gorgeously. As the sun sinks it shines on the inside face of the stained-glass windows, deadening the images in the coloured glass. The interpretation is clear. The legendary Gospels are more colourful but less illuminating than the austere message of contemporary criticism; but the clarity brought by the new learning enables the worshippers not only to see more clearly the world immediately around them, but to have a more natural and less fractured vision of the source of light in God himself.

Though this message is plain, the poem operates at more than one level, and is more carefully crafted than a first reading might suggest. It is one of Clough's earliest metrical experiments, and the variation in the length of the lines is highly successful in producing a number of effects. The underlying rhythm is that of the pentameter; where feet are missing this makes the rhyme, arriving sooner than expected, reverberate. Thus, 'gone' echoes mournfully through the missing feet in the second line, to be answered by the more hopeful echo in the short line, which provides the *peripete* of the poem, 'However'. Couplets whose second line is longer give a sense of accelerando; couplets with a shorter second line force a rallentando. This enables the poet to alternate moments of excitement with moments of more sober reflection – matching the different modes of religious experience symbolized by the two kinds of glass.

The poem does not suggest that the glories of the Gospels are departed for ever; indeed, it holds out hope of some yet unforeseen synthesis to come between the naïve Gospel message and the sophistication of criticism. But after the 'however' we are given a

76

sober heroic couplet which could belong to a poet of the age of reason, before a final alexandrine puts the poem to bed by turning the couplet into a triplet.

The title of the poem indicates a further level of meaning. *Epi-Strauss-ion* is clearly modelled on a Greek word; but there are in fact two words whose pattern it fits: *epitaphion* or epitaph, and *epithalamion* or epithalamium. The poem is in fact both at the same time. It is an epitaph for the evanished Evangelists; but it is also an epithalamium for the union of divine wisdom and human scholarship. In Psalm 19 the divine law is compared with the sun which God has set in the sky,

> Which is as a bridegroom coming out of his chamber, and rejoiceth as a strong man to run a race. His going forth is from the end of the heaven, and his circuit unto the ends of it: and there is nothing hid from the heat thereof.

The circuit of the Son from rising to setting is the symbol of the progressive divine revelation, first through the primitive gorgeousness of the evangelical legends, now through the more austere maturity of nineteenth-century critical thought. The last line of Clough's poem echoes the first line of the psalm: the heavens show forth the glory of God.

Clough welcomed contemporary higher criticism, and professed that it was no threat to the essence of Christianity. But he was not similarly comfortable with another element in the spirit of the age, namely the materialism and determinism which some saw as intrinsic to the scientific temper. In the letter earlier quoted to his sister he wrote: 'The thing which men must work at, will not be critical questions about the scriptures, but philosophical problems of Grace and Free will' (C: 182).

Materialist determinism he saw as, among other things, a threat to the individuality and authority of the poet. Clough's contribution to *Ambarvalia* ends with an affirmation of the poet's right to question this devaluation of his own gift. In the poem 'Is it true, ye gods, who treat us', he asks:

> *Is it true that poetical power*
> *The gift of heaven, the dower,*
> *Of Apollo and the Nine,*
> *The inborn sense, 'the vision and the faculty divine',*
> *All we glorify and bless*
> *In our rapturous exaltation,*

> *All invention and creation,*
> *Exuberance of fancy, and sublime imagination,*
> *All a poet's fame is built on,*
> *The fame of Shakespeare, Milton,*
> *Of Wordsworth, Byron, Shelley,*
> *Is in reason's grave precision,*
> *Nothing more, nothing less,*
> *Than a peculiar conformation,*
> *Constitution, and condition,*
> *Of the brain and of the belly?*

(P: 42)

He does not dare to answer this with a definite 'no'. Perhaps the gods are cheating us, and if a God cheats he cheats thoroughly. (He seems to have toyed with the title 'Wenn Gott betrugt ist wohl betrogen'.) Those who believe this, though, should say so openly; and the poet reserves his own right to doubt: 'It may be, and yet be not.'

So much, then, for the relationship between materialism and poetry. The relationship between deterministic science and religion is explored in an earlier poem in the same collection, 'When Israel Came Out of Egypt', later changed to *The New Sinai*. The theme of this poem is that the scientific scepticism of the age is a stage in the fuller revelation of God. The poet describes how mankind in its infancy had chased idols and false gods. Moses, disappearing into the dark cloud on Sinai, had brought the revelation of the one true God who spoke out of thunder:

> *God spake it out, 'I, God, am One';*
> *The unheeding ages ran,*
> *And baby-thoughts again, again*
> *Have dogged the growing man;*
> *And as of old from Sinai's top*
> *God said that God is One,*
> *By Science strict so speaks He now*
> *To tell us, There is None!*
> *Earth goes by chemic forces; Heaven's*
> *A Mécanique Céleste*
> *And heart and mind of human kind*
> *A watch-work as the rest!*
>
> *Is this a Voice, as was the Voice*
> *Whose speaking told abroad,*
> *When thunder pealed and mountain reeled*

> *The ancient truth of God?*
> *Ah, not the Voice; 'tis but the cloud*
>   *The outer darkness dense,*
> *Where image none, nor e'er was seen*
>   *Similitude of sense.*
> *'Tis but the cloudy darkness dense*
>   *That wrapt the Mount around;*
> *When in amaze the people stays*
>   *To hear the Coming Sound.*
>
> *Some chosen prophet-soul the while*
>   *Shall dare, sublimely meek,*
> *Within the shroud of blackest cloud*
>   *The Deity to seek:*
> *Mid atheistic systems dark*
>   *And darker hearts' despair,*
> *That soul has heard perchance His word,*
>   *And on the dusky air*
> *His skirts, as passed He by, to see*
>   *Hath strained on their behalf*
> *Who on the plain, with dance amain,*
>   *Adore the Golden Calf.*
>
> *'Tis but the cloudy darkness dense*
>   *Though blank the tale it tells*
> *No God, no Truth! Yet He, in sooth,*
>   *Is there – within it dwells;*
> *Within the sceptic darkness deep*
>   *He dwells that none may see,*
> *Till idol forms and idol thoughts*
>   *Have passed and ceased to be.*

(P: 18–19)

The moral was that one should neither relapse, like the Puseyites, into the infantile idolatry of the Golden Calf, nor accept the current atheism of science as the last word from the mystic mountain. Mankind should neither reject science, nor embrace superstition, but wait in faith for God to complete His plan of revelation.

The New Sinai stands out in *Ambarvalia* because of its use of the Bible; not only the setting and the dominant image but also many verbal details in each verse are taken from the Book of Exodus. As Clough ceased to believe in the literal truth of the Bible, he began to place an increasing value on it as a poetic expression of eternal truths. In the years 1847–50 much of his poetry is very closely welded to biblical texts. We have already seen an example of this in *Bethesda*. To this period too belong a series of poems dramatizing scenes from Genesis, such as *Jacob's Wives*, a marvellous antiphonal characterization of the passionate Rachel and the matronly Leah; *Jacob*, a death-bed monologue which is the least successful of these poems; and *Genesis XXIV*, a ballad-like rendering of the story of Isaac and Rebecca. *The Song of Lamech* takes one of the most cryptic and unpromising verses in the Bible, 'And Lamech said unto his wives Adah and Zillah, hearken unto my speech: for I have slain a man to my wounding and a young man to my hurt', and turns it into a long and moving lyric about repentance and reconciliation. The densest and most fully developed of Clough's meditations on Genesis is the unfinished dramatic dialogue *Adam and Eve*, which will be considered in another chapter.

Even in *The Bothie*, which in general, of set purpose, avoids religious topics, there is evidence of Clough's new awareness of the poetic potentiality of biblical quotation and allusion. It was the feature of the poem which most struck Hawkins when it came into his hands. He wrote, in February 1849:

> Will you excuse my telling you that I have been reading your poem 'The Bothie etc.' and cannot but say that what I was told of it was true, that there are parts of it rather indelicate; and I very much regretted to find also that there were frequent allusions to Scripture, or rather parodies of Scripture, which you should not have put forth.
>
> (C: 247)

It is difficult to locate the passages which shocked Hawkins, and no doubt he was oversensitive. But it is true that Clough's new critical attitude to the Bible made him feel free to use its text in irreverent and sometimes blasphemous ways – though often for purposes which he would certainly have regarded as totally moral, and indeed religious. *The New Decalogue*, which is too well known to need quotation here, is an excellent example of the satiric use of biblical language to give savage point to a moral message.

The most extreme example of the liberties which Clough took with the sacred text is a parody of parts of the Vulgate text of the Apocalypse which is preserved in a manuscript in the Bodleian Library. This has never been published, but if Hawkins had ever seen it, it would have confirmed all his worst suspicions about the sad condition of the poet's soul. The manuscript bears the title: *Addenda ad Apocalypsin secundum interpretationem vulgatam.* Its satiric impact is powerful, and even today anyone accustomed to the Vulgate as a sacred and liturgical text is bound to read it with a sense of shock. In the translation which follows, I have endeavoured to render quotations and echoes from the Vulgate into quotations and echoes from the Authorized Version:

> And the spirit said unto me, These things are dreams.
>
> And it said, I am the Spirit, that is I am nothing; I have no Body, that is, substance.
>
> And it said unto me, See, this is my sister Pandemia who has body and flesh and limbs and substance. Come, take her and lie with her. For with me no man can lie. And the Spirit and the Virgin said Come.
>
> And I stood in the desert, in Babylon, in the streets of the ways of Babylon, and I opened my arms, and I bared my loins, and I cried and said, Come holy Pandemia, behold thy servant, be it done according to thy will.
>
> And there stood before my face a woman slender and tall, of about thirty years of age. And she said unto me
>
> I am Pandemia whom thou seekest.
>
> Lo, I am not spirit, I have body and flesh and limbs and substance. Blessed are those that lie with me.
>
> And she said, I am the life, and the way and the truth. He who taketh me doth not walk in the darkness; he who is without me is wholly in darkness and dare not either do good nor evil; those who possess me both possess the world and are not overcome by the world.
>
> He who fears to come to me doth not know where he is, and doth not know even whether he is. [Dare] to come to me and ye shall have life.
>
> And she said, what thou dost, do quickly.
>
> And I cried, and I wept, and I said,
>
> O my lady, I am spirit; I cannot lie with body and flesh.
>
> And she placed her hand on my shoulder and said, Come, and try, and see.
>
> And I lifted up my hands and threw me on the ground and cried with a great cry and said
>
> O Lord, my God, who has made both body and soul and spirit, help me.
>
> And there was silence.

And the woman said, try, and see.

And there was silence, in heaven and on the earth, for about the space of one day.

And in the evening I lifted up my face and I looked and I saw a woman dressed in white clothings, and she came to me and held up my hand and said, I am thy fellow servant, the servant of the Most High who is the creator of all things whatsoever there are.

Come, let us serve together, you and I, and let us help one another.

And I looked into her face and I said

Art thou not that Pandemia whom I called upon and who spake unto me?

And she said, I am thy fellow servant, the servant of the Most High. Let us serve together, you and I. Come.

And the Spirit and the Virgin said, Come. This is a great mystery. Blessed are they that have ears to hear, and hear.

It is not easy to know what to make of this pastiche of New Testament passages. Who is Pandemia? Is she to be identified, as suggested by R. K. Biswas, with the Eros Pandemos or vulgar Aphrodite of Plato's *Symposium* – Profane love as opposed to Sacred? (Biswas: 182–3) Perhaps she is an anticipation of the spirit of worldliness in *Dipsychus*. But why is the whole written in the Latin of the Vulgate? Perhaps Clough thought that the parody was something too blasphemous to be brought out of the decent obscurity of a learned language even in the privacy of a notebook. That he meant the work to be shocking is clear from the title *Addenda ad Apocalypsin*. It is an allusion to the verses which conclude the Book of Revelation: 'For I testify unto every man that heareth the words of the prophecy of this book, if any man shall add unto these things, God shall add unto him the plagues that are written in this book.' The poet's irreverent postscript seems almost an invocation of this threat, like Bertrand Russell's challenge to God to prove His existence by striking him dead.

The most successful of Clough's attempts to use biblical language for poetical purposes, indeed the most powerful of all his purely religious poems, is *Easter Day*, which he wrote during his Italian sojourn in 1849. The poem begins with a passionate denial of the Resurrection of Christ, couched in the words in which it is proclaimed in the final chapters of the Gospels and in the fifteenth chapter of the first Epistle to the Corinthians:

Through the great sinful streets of Naples as I past,
With fiercer heat than flamed above my head
My heart was hot within me; till at last
My brain was lightened, when my tongue had said,
  Christ is not risen!

 Christ is not risen, no,
 He lies and moulders low;
  Christ is not risen.

What though the stone were rolled away, and though
 The grave found empty there –
 If not there, then elsewhere;
If not where Joseph laid Him first, why then
 Where other men
Translaid Him after; in some humbler clay
 Long ere today
Corruption that sad perfect work hath done,
Which here she scarcely, lightly had begun.
 The foul engendered worm
Feeds on the flesh of the life-giving form
Of our most Holy and Anointed One.

 He is not risen, no
 He lies and moulders low;
  Christ is not risen.

 Ashes to ashes, dust to dust;
 As of the unjust, also of the just –
  Christ is not risen.

What if the women, ere the dawn was grey,
Saw one or more great angels, as they say,
Angels, or Him, himself? Yet neither there, nor then
Nor afterward, nor elsewhere, nor at all,
Hath he appeared to Peter or the Ten,
Nor, save in thunderous terror, to blind Saul;
Save in an after-Gospel and late Creed
 He is not risen indeed,
  Christ is not risen.

        (P: 199)

From the beginning the poem sets itself the task of stating, in as concrete terms as possible, what is involved in denying the Resurrection of Jesus. As the poem progresses, it states alternative accounts to explain the Gospel stories, and draws out the consequences of the non–occurrence of the Resurrection for the life of would-be Christians.

If Jesus did not die, then his body has long since rotted. If the Gospel story of the empty tomb is true, that can mean only that Jesus' body was moved elsewhere, to some less honoured grave, where it has long since been eaten by worms. To Jesus' body, just like that of any other human, saint or sinner, there can be applied the words of the burial service: ashes to ashes, and dust to dust. The stories of appearances of Jesus to disciples after his death are no doubt all false. But the next stanza alleges that, even if they were true accounts of experience, they do not involve a genuine rising from the dead. After all, as St Matthew himself tells us, some even of the original disciples doubted the story (Matthew 28: 17):

> Or what if e'en, as runs the tale, the Ten
> Saw, heard and touched, again and yet again?
> What if at Emmaus' inn and by Capernaum's lake
>   Came One the bread that brake,
> Came One that spake as never mortal spake,
> And with them ate and drank and stood and walked about?
>   Ah! 'some' did well to 'doubt'!
> Ah! the true Christ, while these things came to pass,
> Nor heard, nor spake, nor walked, nor dreamt, alas!
>   He was not risen, no,
>   He lay and mouldered low,
>   Christ was not risen.

In that verse the poem appears to countenance the idea that the Resurrection appearances may have been in some way veridical, but yet were not incompatible with the tomb not being empty. This supposition, though in Clough's day no doubt quite incompatible with an Oxford fellowship, has not, in our own day, prevented those who hold it from promotion to episcopacy. Next, the poem suggests the kind of explanation given by critical historians of how the false story of the Resurrection may have gained credence:

> As circulates in some great city crowd
> A rumour changeful, vague, importunate, and loud
> From no determined centre, or of fact,
>   Or authorship exact,
>   Which no man can deny
>   Nor verify;

So spread the wondrous fame;
He all the same
Lay senseless, mouldering, low.
He was not risen, no,
 Christ was not risen!

Ashes to ashes, dust to dust;
As of the unjust, also of the just –
Yea, of that Just One too.
This is the one sad Gospel that is true,
 Christ is not risen.

In the second part, the poem, having hitherto contradicted the Gospel message, now reverses the message of St Paul's Epistle to the Corinthians. St Paul wrote:

Now if Christ be preached that he rose from the dead, how say some among you that there is no resurrection of the dead? But if there be no resurrection of the dead, then is Christ not risen:

And if Christ be not risen, then is our preaching vain, and your faith is also vain. . . .

If in this life only we have hope in Christ, we are of all men most miserable.

Clough takes St Paul's argument with total seriousness. But unlike St Paul he does not take it as a *reductio ad absurdum* argument from the impossibility of Christ's not having risen to the impossibility of denying the future resurrection of mankind. Instead, he accepts each stage of the argument as a true proposition: Christ is not risen, we shall not rise, we are of all men the most miserable. We can apply to ourselves the words which Jesus spoke to the women who sought to comfort him on his way to Calvary:

Weep not for me, but for yourselves and for your children. For behold, the days are coming in the which they shall say Blessed are the barren, and the wombs that never bare, and the paps which never gave suck. Then shall they begin to say to the mountains, Fall on us; and to the hills, Cover us.

        (Luke 23: 29–30)

Is He not risen, and shall we not rise?
 Oh, we unwise!
What did we dream, what wake we to discover?

85

> *Ye hills, fall on us, and ye mountains, cover!*
> *In darkness and great gloom*
> *Come ere we thought it is* our *day of doom,*
> *From the cursed world which is one tomb,*
> *Christ is not risen!*
>
> *Eat, drink, and die, for we are men deceived,*
> *Of all the creatures under heaven's wide cope*
> *We are most hopeless who had once most hope,*
> *We are most wretched that had most believed.*
> *Christ is not risen.*
>
> *Eat, drink, and play, and think that this is bliss!*
> *There is no Heaven but this!*
> *There is no Hell;*
> *Save Earth, which serves the purpose doubly well,*
> *Seeing it visits still*
> *With equallest apportionments of ill*
> *Both good and bad alike, and brings to one same dust*
> *The unjust and the just*
> *With Christ, who is not risen.*

At the line 'Save Earth, which serves the purpose doubly well' the poem, for the first and only time, momentarily indulges in irony. The lightening of tone is welcome amid the hammer-beat of brazen denial. But the lightened tone brings no softening of the message; and in the next stanza we return to the full sad Gospel. Ecclesiastes told us that for men there is no better thing under the sun than to eat, and drink, and be merry; but for cheated Christians there is no room for merriment:

> *Eat, drink, and die, for we are souls bereaved,*
> *Of all the creatures under this broad sky*
> *We are most hopeless, that had hoped most high,*
> *And most beliefless, that had most believed.*
> *Ashes to ashes, dust to dust*
> *As of the unjust, also of the just –*
> *Yea, of that Just One too.*
> *It is the one sad Gospel that is true,*
> *Christ is not risen.*

What, then, should we do? Service to the dead Christ must be replaced by service to our living neighbours; idle gazing into heaven must give way to workday life. Jesus' own teaching, now that he

86

has not risen, is shown as delusive. His disciples must forget the promise to make them fishers of men which caused them to forsake their nets (Mark 1: 17–8); forget the exhortation in the Sermon on the Mount, 'Lay not up for yourselves treasures upon earth, where moth and rust doth corrupt, and where thieves break through and steal; but lay up for yourselves treasures in heaven' (Matthew 6: 19–20):

> *Weep not beside the Tomb,*
> *Ye women, unto whom*
> *He was great solace while ye tended Him;*
> *Ye who with napkin o'er His head*
> *And folds of linen round each wounded limb*
> *Laid out the Sacred Dead;*
> *And thou that bar'st Him in thy Wondering Womb.*
> *Yea, Daughters of Jerusalem, depart,*
> *Bind up as best ye may your own sad bleeding heart;*
> *Go to your homes, your living children tend,*
> *Your earthly spouses love;*
> *Set your affections* not *on things above.*
> *Which moth and rust corrupt, which quickliest come to end:*
> *Or pray, if pray ye must, and pray, if pray ye can,*
> *For death; since dead is He whom ye deemed more than man,*
> *Who is not risen, no,*
> *But lies and moulders low,*
> *Who is not risen.*
>
> *Ye men of Galilee!*
> *Why stand ye looking up to heaven, where Him ye ne'er may see,*
> *Neither ascending hence, nor hither returning again?*
> *Ye ignorant and idle fishermen!*
> *Hence to your huts and boats and inland native shore,*
> *And catch not men, but fish*
> *Whate'er things ye might wish.*
> *Him neither here nor there ye e'er shall meet with more.*
> *Ye poor deluded youths, go home,*
> *Mend the old nets ye left to roam,*
> *Tie the split oar, patch the torn sail;*
> *It was indeed 'an idle tale'.*
> *He was not risen.*

In the twentieth chapter of St John doubting Thomas is brought to acknowledge the divinity of the risen Christ. Jesus replies to him,

'Thomas, because thou hast seen me, thou hast believed: blessed are
they that have not seen and yet have believed.' This message too
must be reversed:

> *And oh, good men of ages yet to be,*
> *Who shall believe because ye did not see,*
> *   Oh, be ye warned! be wise!*
> *   No more with pleading eyes,*
> *   And sobs of strong desire,*
> *Unto the empty vacant void aspire,*
> *Seeking another and impossible birth*
> *That is not of your own and only Mother Earth.*
> *But if there is no other life for you,*
> *Sit down and be content, since this must even do;*
> *   He is not risen.*
>
> *   One look, and then depart,*
> *   Ye humble and ye holy men of heart!*
> *And ye! ye ministers and stewards of a word*
> *Which ye would preach, because another heard, –*
> *   Ye worshippers of that ye do not know,*
> *   Take these things hence and go;*
> *   He is not risen.*

Christian ministers are in no better case than the superstitious
Athenians rebuked by Paul for ignorantly worshipping an unknown God (Acts 17: 23), or the traffickers in the Temple to whom
Jesus said, 'Take these things hence; make not my Father's house an
house of merchandise':

> *   Here on our Easter Day*
> *We rise, we come, and lo! we find Him not;*
> *   Gardener nor other on the sacred spot,*
> *Where they have laid Him is there none to say!*
> *No sound, nor in, nor out; no word*
> *Of where to seek the dead or meet the living Lord;*
> *There is no glistering of an angel's wings,*
> *There is no voice of heavenly clear behest:*
> *Let us go hence, and think upon these things*
> *In silence, which is best.*
> *   Is he not risen? No –*
> *   But lies and moulders low –*
> *   Christ is not risen.*

More than any other of Clough's poems, *Easter Day* speaks with equal strength to believers and to unbelievers alike. It speaks to, and for, unbelievers because of its unqualified, unblinking denial of the central doctrine of Christianity. It speaks to believers because of its whole-hearted acceptance of the importance of what is denied and its unflinching vision of the hopes which are given up by one who abandons Christianity. This compelling power is derived, more than anything else, by the skill with which Clough uses the Gospel's own language to negate the Gospel's prime message.

Some who have read the poem carefully have indeed taken it, not at its face value, but as an actual exhortation to faith. The Christless world is portrayed as so unbearably bleak, it has been argued, that the poet is inviting the reader to ask himself, 'Can I face a world as horrible as that?' and to give the answer no. Taken out of its context, the poem could indeed support that reading; but knowing its place in Clough's intellectual history, such an interpretation seems unlikely. Yet Clough himself, speaking later in the voice of Dipsychus, was to say of the poem: 'Interpret it I cannot. I but wrote it.'

Hopkins, unlike Clough, seems to have been totally untouched by the impact of higher criticism on the traditional acceptation of the Bible. Throughout his life, he accepted the Bible as literally inspired, and as a consequence of this he regarded its historical narratives as an unimpeachable record of events. If some narrative in the Bible seemed implausible, the way to respond to this was not to question whether it was truly in a historical genre, still less to call in doubt the Bible's inerrancy, but rather to invent elaborate hypotheses to explain how what was described in the Bible might actually have happened. A remarkable example of this is to be found in one of Hopkins's very last writings, some notes which he made in a retreat in Ireland in January 1888.

On 6 January, the Feast of the Epiphany, he noted that he had received 'ever so much light on the mystery of the feast and the historical interpretation of the gospel'. He committed this to several pages of notes, which include the following account of Herod's dealing with the Magi:

He sent them to Bethlehem, that is sent a guide to show the road, courtesy so requiring. Writers ask why did he not send someone to report where they went. There could be a difficulty: it must be secretly, and from them. He could not commit himself by any known messenger; he would then seem to be recognising the Pretender. In the urgency he might not find a secret follower, and he thought there was no need. Then probably they do not enter Bethlehem. The stable was outside. The Bethlehemites saw little of them, did not know where they went. They would encamp near the spot and the dream was that very night; they set out before morning, and Herod altogether lost sight of them.

Herod had meant to say on their return, that they were mistaken, this could not be the expected King, etc., and afterwards to treat the matter as a conspiracy. No doubt he still more treated it so when he found himself 'mocked'. He probably does not act at once, but waits some weeks or months for a pretext, for the conspiracy to show itself. But the Bethlehemites had no plot and little knowledge on the subject. There was the story of the shepherds, but, so to say, nothing had followed it. After the Purification the Holy Family had probably disappeared. Herod of course availed himself of the registration and found St Joseph's name and place of abode, and so marked out Christ for death; but not as a likely, rather as an unlikely case. For by enquiring at Nazareth it would have appeared that the birth of Joseph's child at Bethlehem must have been a chance (and no doubt they had stayed at home till the last date possible), so that there could not well have been a plot. When Herod acted at last he must have pretended a conspiracy, required a confession, and getting none made this proof of general guilt, and so justified a general slaughter.

(S: 255–6)

If we compare the use of the Bible by Hopkins to its use by Clough, we meet with a paradox in Hopkins's life which is a mirror image of one we noticed in that of Clough. Clough began to use the Bible to the greatest poetic effect only after he had begun to lose faith in its inspiration. By contrast, Hopkins's use of the Bible was most exuberant before his conversion to Catholicism, and dwindled to very modest proportions once he had become a Jesuit. In Clough's case, free poetical exploitation of biblical material was possible only after he had freed himself from belief in its literal inspiration. In the case of Hopkins, we have to look elsewhere for the explanation of the phenomenon.

The fragments of the youthful poem *Pilate* include a poetic presentation of the scene in which Pilate washes his hands as he yields, at the trial of Christ, to the clamour for crucifixion. But the biblical material is interwoven with allusions to the legend that Pilate's body rests amid the glacial slopes of Mount Pilatus near Lucerne.

More austerely biblical, from Hopkins's first year at Balliol, is *A Soliloquy of one of the Spies left in the Wilderness*. This is in a genre very similar to the Old Testament poems of Clough; it treats a scene in Exodus as Clough treated several passages in Genesis. The Book of Exodus reports that the Israelites led out of Egypt by Moses complained constantly about the hardships of the migration, and called in question their leader's authority. For instance:

> And the whole congregation of the children of Israel murmured against Moses and Aaron in the wilderness: And the children of Israel said unto them, Would to God we had died by the hand of the Lord in the land of Egypt, when we sat by the flesh pots and when we did eat bread to the full; for ye have brought us into this wilderness, to kill this whole assembly with hunger.
>
> (Exodus 16: 2–4)

In the ten stanzas of the *Soliloquy* of which the following are samples, Hopkins dramatizes the murmuring of the Israelites:

> *Who is this Moses? Who made him, we say,*
> *To be a judge and ruler over us?*
> *He slew the Egyptian yesterday. Today*
> *   In hot sands perilous*
> *He hides our corpses dropping by the way*
> *   Wherein he makes us stray.*
>
> *Your hands have borne the tent-poles: on you plod:*
> *The trumpet waxes loud: tired are your feet.*
> *Come by the flesh-pots: you shall sit unshod*
> *   And have your fill of meat;*
> *Bring wheat-ears from the loamy stintless sod,*
> *   To a more grateful god.*
>
> (O: 23)

Crucial for the understanding of Hopkins's poetic attitude to the Bible is *Barnfloor and Winepress*. This was printed in *The Union Review* in 1865. Its title alludes to a verse from the second Book of Kings, which is quoted as a motto. The verse occurs in a description of a terrible famine in Samaria, in which asses' heads and doves' dung were being sold for many silver pieces:

And as the king of Israel was passing by upon the wall there cried a woman unto him, saying, Help, my lord, O king. And he said, if the Lord do not help thee, whence shall I help thee? Out of the barnfloor, or out of the winepress? And the king said unto her, What aileth thee? And she answered, This woman said unto me, Give thy son, that we may eat him today, and we will eat my son tomorrow. So we boiled my son and did eat him: and I said unto her on the next day, Give thy son, that we may eat him; and she hath hid her son. And it came to pass, when the king heard the words of the woman, that he rent his clothes.

(II Kings 6: 26–30)

In Hopkins's poem this gruesome story is not explicitly exploited; instead, the King's words are made the text for a meditation on the Eucharist, contrasting the empty barnfloor and the dry winepress with the heavenly bread and wine upon the altar:

> *Thou that on sin's wages starvest,*
> *Behold we have the joy in harvest:*
> *For us was gather'd the first fruits,*
> *For us was lifted from the roots,*
> *Sheaved in cruel bands, bruised sore,*
> *Scourged upon the threshing floor;*
> *Where the upper mill-stone roof'd His head*
> *At morn we found the heavenly Bread,*
> *And, on a thousand altars laid,*
> *Christ our Sacrifice is made!*
>
> *Thou whose dry plot for moisture gapes,*
> *We shout with them that tread the grapes:*
> *For us the Vine was fenced with thorn,*
> *Five ways the precious branches torn;*
> *Terrible fruit was on the tree*
> *In the acre of Gethsemane;*
> *For us by Calvary's distress*
> *The wine was racked from the press;*
> *Now in our altar-vessels stored*
> *Is the sweet Vintage of the Lord.*

(O: 26)

In these two stanzas the biblical allusions are woven through and across each other in a rich texture. The New Testament account of Jesus' arrest, binding, scourging, crowning with thorns, and

92

fivefold wounding is described first in the image of the crushing of wheat into bread, and then in the image of the pressing of grapes into wine. The description of the wheat and grape harvest is couched in Old Testament language, not only by reference to the overarching text, but through line-by-line allusion to particular passages. Thus, there are echoes of the song of the vineyard in Isaiah 5 (the hedge will be taken away and there shall come up thorns), the joy in harvest that will come when the people that walked in darkness see a great light (Isaiah 9: 3), the first fruits which the Torah commanded to be offered to God (Leviticus 2: 12, etc), and the winepress of the wrath of God from which blood flooded out (Revelations 14: 19–20). Finally, the context of the motto provides a remarkable piece of typology. Just as the starving people of Samaria relieve their hunger by eating the son of an Israelite woman, so the contemporary Christian relieves his spiritual hunger by eating the flesh of the Galilean maiden's son. The cannibalistic overtones of the poem are in their way as shocking as the carnal ones of Clough's *Addenda*.

This poem was one of the last written by Hopkins as an Anglican. The richness of its allusive use of the Authorized Version caused him some problems when he became a Roman Catholic, because of the Catholic prohibition on using vernacular versions of the Bible which had not been made from the Latin Vulgate. In January 1867 he promised to send a copy of the poem to his friend E. W. Urquhart. By 15 August he had still not sent it, and he explained in a letter:

> Such an absurd little hindrance prevents my sending you *Barnfloor and Winepress*: there are quotations or quasi-quotations from the Bible in it and I must check them by the Douay before I can reproduce the verses, but a Douay I have not got.
>
> (L, III: 41)

The result was that he thoroughly recast the poem, though he admitted in a later letter that as a version of the Bible the Douay was inferior to the Authorized Version.

The embarrassment of feeling obliged by ecclesiastical law to make use of an English version which he knew to be inferior may be one reason why, in Hopkins's Catholic poetry, allusions to the Bible are rarer, and less explicit, than they were in his Anglican poetry. Another reason, also illustrated by *Barnfloor and Winepress* itself, is that sacramental symbolism and liturgical language became for him, as vehicles for the expression of religious emotion, more important than the language of either the Old or the New Testaments.

Even in his Anglican days, as *Pilate* illustrates, Hopkins was attracted by legendary embroideries of the Bible story. He was later often moved by the writings of modern mystics such as Sister Emmerich and Marie Lataste claiming to have received revelations supplementing the Bible. The legends of the Saints were also an important vehicle of poetic expression, as witness the several versions of lines on a picture of St Dorothea, the poems in praise of St Paul's legendary disciple St Thecla, and the late ambitious project for a drama about St Winifred. In Hopkins's poetry allusions to sacramental ritual, liturgical texts, and hagiographical legends well outnumber biblical references. Even his early Easter poems, for instance, are not really, like *Easter Day*, about Christ's Resurrection but rather about the ending of the Lenten fast (*Easter Communion*) or the celebration of the Easter liturgy (*Easter*).

Biblical allusions are not, of course, absent from Hopkins's Catholic poetry, but they tend to become more deeply encrypted in the text. A study of *The Wreck of the Deutschland* reveals few lines that at all resemble explicit quotation. There are, however, a number of passages which make fine use of biblical material. In the first stanza, for instance, we read:

> *Thou hast bound bones and veins in me, fastened me flesh*
> *And after it almost unmade, what with dread,*
> *Thy doing: and dost thou touch me afresh?*

> (O: 110)

This echoes a striking passage in the Book of Job:

> Remember, I beseech thee, that thou has made me as the clay; and wilt thou bring me into dust again? . . . Thou hast clothed me with skin and flesh, and hast fenced me with bones and sinews.

> (Job 10:9, 11, AV)

In the same poem the image 'I steady as a water in a well' (O: 111) recalls the promise made by Jesus in St John (4: 14) that the disciple would have within himself a well of water springing up into everlasting life. The prophetic cry of the tall nun in the shipwreck is contrasted with the despair of the disciples in the storm on Gennesareth (Matthew 8: 3–25). The references to God the Father's 'feathers' and the description of Luther as 'beast of the waste wood' recall passages in the Psalter (91: 4; 80: 13, AV) which Hopkins would have encountered weekly, in Latin, as part of his recitation of the divine office. St Paul tells us (I Corinthians 2: 9), 'eye hath not seen, nor ear heard, neither have entered into the heart of man, the things which God hath prepared for them that love him'. So Hopkins defines 'the heaven of desire' as 'the treasure never eyesight got, nor was ever guessed what for the hearing' (O: 116).

Scholars have devotedly combed the text of *The Wreck of the Deutschland* for biblical allusion and parallel. If we leave out far-fetched allusions, the harvest is surprisingly small. Of course there are many references to religious doctrines and practices which a Catholic would claim to trace to an original authority in the Bible. But that is something different from the poetic use of language drawn from the Bible which is so effective in the late Clough and the early Hopkins.

Only towards the end of his life, with the sonnets of desolation, does Hopkins return to the rich biblical allusiveness of his youth. Parts of *Carrion Comfort* are almost as tightly woven from biblical texts as *Barnfloor and Winepress*. The depression of his last days made him turn to Jeremiah. 'Righteous art thou, O Lord, when I plead with thee; yet let me talk with thee of thy judgments: Wherefore doth the way of the wicked prosper?' (Jeremiah 12: 1). He placed this text, in Latin, as the epigraph for one of the finest of the despondent sonnets, which begins:

> *Thou art indeed just, Lord, if I contend*
> *With thee; but, sir, so what I plead is just.*
> *Why do sinners' ways prosper? and why must*
> *Disappointment all I endeavour end?*

(O: 183)

Amid the despondency of Hopkins's final poetry, there is one poem of hope, *That Nature is a Heraclitean Fire, and of the comfort of the Resurrection*. The last lines of it make use of the same chapter of First Corinthians (15) which underlay the end of *Easter Day*. They sound out a triumphant rebuff to the hopeless, beliefless pessimism of that poem:

> *Enough! The Resurrection,*
> *A heart's-clarion! Away grief's gasping, joyless days, dejection.*
> *Across my foundering deck shone*
> *A beacon, an eternal beam. Flesh fade, and mortal trash*

Fall to the residuary worm; world's wildfire, leave but ash:
  In a flash, at a trumpet crash,
I am all at once what Christ is, since he was what I am, and
This Jack, joke, poor potsherd, patch, matchwood, immortal diamond
  Is immortal diamond.

7

THE MYSTERY OF THE FALL

Clough made several attempts to present biblical material as symbolic expression of eternal truths about the nature and destiny of humanity. The most ambitious was a verse drama printed in the collected poems under the title *Adam and Eve*. It was first published in 1869 under the title *The Mystery of the Fall*, pieced together by Mrs Clough from four MS notebooks and several separate sheets. The drama is unfinished, and the order of its scenes is conjectural; it is not always easy to know whether some scenes are meant as alternatives or as successors to each other. But even in its fragmentary form, the drama is imposing, and contains some of the most moving religious verse Clough ever wrote.

Hopkins, too, devoted much attention to the primeval Fall; indeed, whenever he went through the *Spiritual Exercises* of St Ignatius he was obliged to spend part of the first week in meditation on the triple sin (the Fall of angels, of the human race, of the human individual). It is in his commentaries on the *Exercises*, and in his sermons, rather than in his poetry, that we find Hopkins's reconstruction of the Fall. It is paradoxical, but characteristic of the two men, that when the unbeliever Clough wanted to write a verse drama, he chose for dramatization a central biblical text, while the believer Hopkins chose rather the martyrdom of a legendary saint.

Before examining the two authors' treatment of the Fall, it is well to remind ourselves of the words of the biblical narrative; for each author draws a great deal out of even small details of the text. In the second chapter of Genesis, after the formation of man from dust and divine breath, there is the account of God's planting of the garden of Eden, with the tree of life in the midst of the garden, and the tree of knowledge of good and evil:

And the Lord God took the man and put him into the garden of Eden to dress it and to keep it.

And the Lord God commanded the man, saying, Of every tree of the garden thou mayest freely eat:

97

But of the tree of the knowledge of good and evil, thou shalt not eat of it: for in the day that thou eatest thereof thou shalt surely die.

(Genesis 2: 8–9)

There follows the account of the creation of Eve from Adam's rib.

The temptation and Fall themselves are narrated in the third chapter:

Now the serpent was more subtil than any beast of the field which the Lord God had made. And he said unto the woman, Yea, hath God said, ye shall not eat of every tree of the garden?

And the woman said unto the serpent, We may eat of the fruit of the trees of the garden:

But of the fruit of the tree which is in the midst of the garden, God had said, Ye shall not eat of it, neither shall ye touch it, lest ye die.

And the serpent said unto the woman, Ye shall not surely die: For God doth know that in the day ye eat thereof, then your eyes shall be opened, and ye shall be as gods, knowing good and evil.

And when the woman saw that the tree was good for food, and that it was pleasant to the eyes, and a tree to be desired to make one wise, she took of the fruit thereof, and did eat, and gave also unto her husband with her; and he did eat. And the eyes of them both were opened, and they knew that they were naked; and they sewed fig leaves together, and made themselves aprons.

And they heard the voice of the Lord God walking in the garden in the cool of the day: and Adam and his wife hid themselves from the presence of the Lord God amongst the trees of the garden.

And the Lord God called unto Adam and said unto him, Where art thou?

And he said, I heard thy voice in the garden, and I was afraid, because I was naked, and I hid myself.

And he said, Who told thee that thou wast naked? Hast thou eaten of the tree, whereof I commanded thee that thou shouldest not eat?

And the man said, The woman whom thou gavest to be with me she gave me of the tree and I did eat.

> And the Lord God said unto the woman, What is this that thou hast done? And the woman said, The serpent beguiled me, and I did eat.

There follows the curse upon the serpent (he will go on his belly henceforth), the woman (she shall bring forth in sorrow and be ruled by her husband), and the man (he shall labour in the sweat of his brow to make his bread, and he shall return into the dust from which he was taken). The pair are expelled from Eden. 'Adam knew Eve his wife, and she conceived and bare Cain.'

Hopkins accepts this account as literal, historic truth. Reflection on it is for the purpose of making vivid the story, explaining the course of events, clearing up internal incoherences or implausibilities, and drawing moral and religious lessons from the narrative. He took it as his basis for a sermon in January 1880 at St Francis Xavier's, Liverpool, on 'The Fall of God's First Kingdom' (a title, incidentally, which gave offence and was censored by his superiors).

Satan, he says, having fallen himself through pride and self-love, wished to break God's new kingdom on earth; choosing the weakest spot to attack, he tempted the woman:

> He chose his disguise, he spoke by the serpent's mouth; he watched his time, he found Eve alone. And here some say she should have been warned when she heard a dumb beast speaking reason. But of this we cannot be sure: St Basil says that all the birds and beasts spoke in Paradise; not of course that they were not dumb and irrational creatures by nature then as now, but if a black spirit could speak by them so could a white and it may be that the angels made use of them as instruments to sing God's praises and to entertain man. Neither would Satan needlessly alarm the woman, rather than that he would invisibly have uttered voices in the air. But when she heard what the serpent said, *then* she should have taken alarm. So then to listen to a serpent speaking might be no blame, but how came Eve to be alone? For God had said of Adam *It is not good for man to be alone: let us make him a helpmate like himself*; and Eve was without the helpmate not like only but stronger than herself. She was deceived and Adam, as St Paul tells us, was not nor would have been. Then why was Eve alone?
>
> (S: 63)

Before answering this question, Hopkins in a long passage draws a distinction between three kinds of lawful human action. There are those that God commands, those that God simply permits, and those that he does not command but specially approves – works of supererogation, such as hearing mass on a weekday. He then applies this distinction to the case of Adam and Eve as vassal princes of the earth under the sovereignty of God:

> Eve was alone. It was no sin to be alone, she was in her duty, God had given her freedom and she was wandering free, God had made her independent of her husband and she need not be at his side. Only God had made her for Adam's companion; it was her office, her work, the reason of her being to companion him and she was not doing it. There is no sin, but there is no delicacy of duty, no zeal for the sovereign's honour, no generosity, no supererogation. And Adam, he too was alone. He had been commanded to dress and keep Paradise. What flower, what fruitful tree, what living thing was there in Paradise so lovely as Eve, so fruitful as the mother of all flesh, that needed or could repay his tendance and his keeping as she? There was no sin; yet at the one fatal moment when of all the world care was wanted care was not forthcoming, the thing best worth keeping was unkept.
>
> (S: 65)

Hopkins then goes on to rebuke Eve for standing near the fatal tree: not a sinful action, but on the very utmost border of her duty. The temptation itself is described as follows:

> Now, brethren, fancy, as you may, that rich tree all laden with its shining fragrant fruit and swaying down from one of its boughs, as the pythons and great snakes of the East do now, waiting for their prey to pass and then crush it, swaying like a long spray of vine or the bine of a great creeper, not terrible but beauteous, lissome, marked with quaint streaks and eyes or flushed with rainbow colours, the Old Serpent. We must suppose he offered her the fruit, as though it were the homage and the tribute of the brute to man, of the subject to his queen, presented it with his mouth or swept it from the boughs before her feet: and she declined it. Then come those studied words of double meaning the Scripture tells us of: *What! and has God forbidden you to eat of the fruit of Paradise?* – Now mark her answer: you would

expect her to reply: No, but of this one fruit only: he has given us free leave for all the trees in Paradise excepting one – but hear her: *Of the fruit of the trees in Paradise we do eat* – no mention of God's bounty here, it is all their freedom, what they do: 'we do eat' – *but the fruit of the tree in the midst of Paradise* – as if she would say of the best fruit of all – *God has commanded us not to eat of, nor so much as touch it, or we shall die*: then she remembers God when it is a question of a stern and threatening law. She gave her tempter the clew to his temptation – that God her sovereign was a tyrant, a sullen lawgiver; that God her lord and landlord was envious and grudging, a rackrent; that God her father, the author of her being, was a shadow of death.

Hopkins then describes how the serpent acted on this hint, framing his temptation so as to attack God as lawgiver, proprietor, and father. He advises them to trespass boldly on God's rights and seize his crown property. Eve sinned and fell, but God's kingdom was not yet fallen, because it turned on Adam's obedience, not Eve's:

Then came the meeting between the husband and the wife and she learnt that she was deceived and undone. Then her husband must share her lot for better and worse; this selfish and fallen woman would drag her husband in her fall, as she had no thought of God in her innocence, so in her sin she had no charity for her husband: she had so little love for him that she said, if he loved her he must share her lot. Most dearly he loved her, and she stood before him now lovely and her beauty heightened by distress, a thing never seen before in Paradise, herself a Tree of Knowledge of Good and Evil and offering him its fruit; herself a Tree of Life, the mother of all flesh to be. For he thought his hope of offspring would go with her. He was wrong: God, who gave back to Abraham for his obedience his all but sacrificed son, would have given back to Adam for his obedience his fallen wife; but he did not pause to make an act of hope. He listened to her voice. He left his heavenly father and clave to his wife and they two were in one fallen flesh; for her he took the stolen goods and harboured the forfeit person of the thief, rebelling against God, the world's great landlord, owner of earth and man, who had bestowed upon him Paradise.

Hopkins concludes by describing the eviction of the pair from Paradise: 'the judgment of death and the execution of the sentence which we feel yet'.

The sermon is a work of great poetic beauty, and the analysis of the dialogue between Eve and the serpent brings out some delicious nuances in the Genesis story. But Hopkins's fairy-tale, Arabian-nights language must not blind us to the fact that he is treating the story as deadly serious history. In assessing the behaviour of Eve he is like a magistrate looking for mitigating or aggravating circumstances in the conduct of an accused brought before him for contravening the game laws, or a *Times* leader writer summing up the merits and demerits of the measures introduced in Mr Gladstone's second administration. At the present time, to even the most devout Christian reader of the story of the Fall, Hopkins's sermon must seem to be written in a very incongruous register.

Victorians of more critical temper than Hopkins found it difficult to accept Genesis as a historical narrative of a primitive sin committed by an original human pair with grave and enduring consequences for the human race. There were three principal reasons for this.

First, a growing awareness of the differences between different literary genres, and a comparative study of religious writings in other civilizations, made scholars question whether Genesis was ever intended by its original authors to be historical in the sense in which Caesar's or Clarendon's writings are historical. Such questions were raised not only by unbelievers, and authority for raising them could be sought far back in Christian tradition.

Secondly, the chronology which is implied in taking the Old Testament, from beginning to end, as a uniform historical record was incompatible with that suggested by current scientific developments, first of all in geology, and more recently in biology.

Thirdly, the story of the Fall, as interpreted in some passages of St Paul, and in a long tradition of Christian theology, had come to seem even to some Victorian churchmen grossly immoral. Even if it were literally true that the human race were descended from a single pair, and that the first humans had transgressed a mysterious divine command, it seemed cruel and unjust to punish the whole human family for a sin in which all but two of them had had no part.

Clough shared these misgivings about the traditional attitude to the narrative of the Fall. Nevertheless he also felt that the story was a symbolic vehicle for important truths about human nature. *Adam and Eve* explores a number of different ways in which these truths can be dramatized within the fictional context of the Genesis story.

By choosing the dramatic mode of presentation, he avoids the need to make explicit his own disbelief in the historicity of the story. Skilfully, rather than doubting the existence of the historical Adam and Eve, he places the doubts about the Fall narrative in the mouth of Adam himself in the drama.

Clough's play starts the story where Hopkins's sermon left off. The Fall, if Fall there was, is already in the past. Eve, pregnant with Cain, is oppressed with a sense of guilt; as the scene opens she has just been rehearsing the story of the serpent and the forbidden fruit. Adam refuses to accept it; the whole story is a fantasy:

> *What!*
> *Because I plucked an apple from a twig*
> *Be damned to death eterne! parted from Good,*
> *Enchained to Ill! No, by the God of Gods,*
> *No, by the living will within my breast,*
> *It cannot be and shall not . . .*
>
> (P: 165)

> *But thou, poor wife, poor mother, shall I say?*
> *Big with the first maternity of Man,*
> *Draw'st from thy teeming womb thick fancies fond,*
> *That with confusion mix thy delicate brain;*
> *Fondest of which and cloudiest call the dream*
> *(Yea, my beloved, hear me, it is a dream)*
> *Of the serpent and the apple and the curse.*
>
> (P: 166)

Adam now demythologizes the expulsion from Paradise. He remembers how one night in their first home Eve awoke with a nightmare, all because she saw

> *A sly and harmless snake glide by our couch;*
> *And because, some few hours before, a lamb*
> *Fell from a rock and broke its neck, and I*
> *Had answered to your wonder that 'twas dead.*
>
> (P: 167)

He had tried to woo her back to sleep:

> *In vain; for soon*
> *I felt thee gone, and opening widest eyes*
> *Beheld thee kneeling on the turf; hands now*

> *Clenched and uplifted high; now vainly outspread*
> *To hide a burning face and streaming eyes*
> *And pale small lips that muttered faintly 'Death'.*
> *And thou would'st fain depart; thou saidst the place*
> *Was for the likes of us too good: we left*
> *The pleasant woodland shades; and passed abroad*
> *Into this naked champaign, glorious soil*
> *For digging and for delving, but indeed*
> *Until I killed a beast or two, and spread*
> *Skins upon sticks to make our palace here,*
> *A residence sadly exposed to wind and rain.*

> (P: 166)

This pedestrian verse, declining into the language of the estate agent, can hardly be intended to convince the reader. Certainly it does not convince Eve, who presses Adam to confess that they have changed.

Sometimes, Adam concedes, when he trudges weary homeward through dark and storm, it does indeed seem so:

> *I too have lost heart,*
> *And deemed all space with angry power replete,*
> *Angry, almighty; and panic-stricken have cried,*
> *'What have I done? What wilt thou do to me?'*
> *Or with the coward's 'No, I did not, I will not,'*
> *Belied my own soul's self. I too have heard*
> *And listened, too, to a Voice that in my ear*
> *Hissed the temptation to curse God, or worse,*
> *And yet more frequent, curse myself and die.*
> *Until, in fine, I have begun to half-believe*
> *Your dream my dream too, and the dream of both,*
> *No dream but dread reality*

> (P: 167)

When the weeds have choked a season's toil, he has imagined a voice in the sky saying, 'Cursed is the ground for thy sake; thou art cursed.' But he also hears other voices which tell him to put away these childish dreams, to press onward, to live and to grow. But Adam's tale holds no comfort for Eve, who departs with an anguished description of the significance of her pregnancy:

> *The questionings of ages yet to be,*
> *The thinkings and cross-thinkings, self-contempts,*
> *Self-horror; all despondencies, despairs,*

> *Of multitudinous souls on souls to come*
> *In me imprisoned, fight, complain, and cry.*

> (P: 168)

Adam, left alone, is more prepared to countenance the possibility that he has committed some disastrous, irretrievable act. Pangs of remorse alternate with calmer moments in which he dismisses such spasms as idle fits. Sometimes he adopts a poise of detachment from his moods, as 'passing, curious, new phenomena'; sometimes he even sees himself as a mental alchemist, seeking the formula to transmute the drossy contents of his mind into something splendid and magnificent.

Thus first he cries, with limbs convulsed:

> *Fool, fool; where am I? O my God! Fool, fool!*
> *Why did we do't? Eve, Eve! where are you? quick!*
> *His tread is in the garden! Hither it comes!*
> *Hide us, O bushes, and ye thick trees hide!*
> *He comes, on, on. Alack, and all these leaves,*
> *These petty, quivering and illusive blinds,*
> *Avail us nought: the light comes in and in,*
> *Displays us to ourselves; displays, ah, shame,*
> *Unto the inquisitive day our nakedness.*
> *He comes. He calls. The large eye of His truth,*
> *His full, severe, all-comprehending view*
> *Fixes itself upon our guiltiness –*
> *O God, O God, what are we, what shall we be?*

> (P: 169)

These lines are then dismissed, as a passing, if terrible possession. He must note and test all these strange twists of mind; the gift of self-awareness, self-criticism, self-moulding is the one thing preventing him from being a plaything for external forces, material or spiritual:

> *Though tortured in the crucible I lie,*
> *Myself my own experiment, yet still*
> *I, or a something that is I indeed,*
> *A living, central, and more inmost I*
> *Within the scales of mere exterior me's*
> *I – seem eternal, O thou God, as Thou;*
> *Have knowledge of the Evil and the Good,*
> *Superior in a higher Good to both.*

> (P: 169)

The inmost, eternal I seems an uncanny anticipation of the metaphysical ego of Wittgenstein's *Tractatus Logico-Philosophicus* (Kenny: 9). But the alchemist Adam foreshadows many a Faust-like figure; he begins to speak in the accents of the absentminded professor in the grip of an obsession:

> *Really now, had I only time and space,*
> *And were not troubled with this wife of mine,*
> *And the necessity of meat and drink,*
> *I really do believe,*
> *With time and space and proper quietude*
> *I could resolve the problem on my brain.*
> *But no, I scarce can stay one moment more*
> *To watch the curious seething process out.*
> *If I could only dare to let Eve see*
> *These operations, it is like enough*
> *Between us two we two could make it out.*
> *But she would be so frightened, think it proof*
> *Of all her own imaginings.*

(P: 170)

Clough's Adam has had many successors. We are all familiar with the behaviourist, or the biologist, or the neurologist, or the professor of artificial intelligence, who is convinced that a few years, and a sufficiently ample research grant, will enable his department to provide the full and final explanation of the workings of the human mind, and thereby solve the psychological and social problems of the race. Somehow, something always seems to prevent the expected progress; but without such Luciferian ambitions, research might never thrive. As Adam says, in the final speech of the scene:

> *Who loses confidence, he loses all.*
> *A demi-grain of cowardice in me*
> *Avowed were poison to the whole mankind.*
> *When men are plentier 'twill be time to try.*
> *At present, no.*
> *No.*
> *Shake it all up and go.*

(P: 170)

In these first two scenes, Eve is the representative of the traditional myth. Adam, double-minded like all of Clough's heroes, veers between two different attitudes. Sometimes he explains away

Eve's belief as sheer fantasy, and offers pseudo-physiological explanations for her vaporous guilt; at other times, in a more Nietzschean vein, he claims that whatever she is describing as a fall was rather some necessary stage in the development of the human race; in the later words of Dipsychus, 'What we call sin, I could believe a painful opening out of paths for ampler virtue.'

In later scenes, the relationship between the two changes. Eve, though still the more conventionally religious of the two, is prepared to be less emphatic and specific about the Paradisal sin; Adam, though still sceptical about the originating sin, is more pessimistically prepared to admit an inherited sinfulness in future generations. What brings about the change is the birth of Cain, which is narrated in the third scene.

Eve, with her new-born, finds Paradise come back, and her heart in the garden as of old. But Adam looks on the baby Cain with a pessimistic eye. He warns Eve:

> *Hope not too greatly, neither fear for him,*
> *Feeling on thy breast his small compressing lips*
> *And glorying in the gift they draw from thee*
> *Hope not too greatly in thyself and him.*
> *And hear me, O young mother – I must speak.*
> *This child is born of us, and therefore like us*
> *Is born of us, and therefore is as we;*
> *Is born of us, and therefore is not pure;*
> *Earthly, as well as godlike*

(P: 172)

Cain will pass through straits of anguish before coming

> *To the calm ocean which he yet shall reach,*
> *He or himself or in his sons hereafter,*
> *Of consummated consciousness of self.*

(P: 172)

The Christian doctrine of inherited guilt is here engrafted into a Hegelian conception of humanity as a stage in the development of the self-consciousness of spirit.

Adam's sense of Cain's inborn impurity leads to foreboding:

> *The self-same stuff which wrought in us to grief*
> *Runs in his veins; and what to work in him?*
> *What shape of unsuspected deep disguise,*

> *Transcending our experience, our best cares*
> *Baffling, evading all preventive thought,*
> *Will the old mischief choose, I wonder, here?*

(P: 172)

Eve stores up Adam's gloomy words to brood upon. But (in scene IV) she makes a further attempt to persuade Adam that they have been disobedient to God:

> Adam: *Your question's not so simple as it looks;*
> *For if you mean that God said this or that –*
> *As that 'You shall not touch those apples there'*
> *And that we did – why, all that I can say*
> *Is, that I can't conceive the thing to be.*
> *But if it were so, I should then believe*
> *We had done right – at any rate, no harm.*
> Eve: *O Adam, I can scarcely think I hear;*
> *For if God said to us – God being God –*
> *'You shall not' is not His commandment His?*
> *And are not we the creatures He hath made?*
> Adam: *My child, God does not speak to human minds*
> *In that unmeaning arbitrary way;*
> *God were not God, if so, and Good not Good.*

(P: 174)

If Eve were to find in her heart a genuine voice telling her that something is evil, no doubt evil it is; but genuineness is hard to test:

> *God's voice is of the heart: I do not say*
> *All voices, therefore, of the heart are God's;*
> *And to discern the Voice amid the voices*
> *Is the hard task, my love, that we are born to.*

(P: 175)

Eve, borne down now by a sense of disobedience to God, urges Adam to admit that some way, some time, they have done wrong. But even this he is now reluctant to admit, and he is determined that the story of the Fall shall not reach their children.

The remainder of the drama takes place some years later, and its theme the murder of Abel by Cain. Again, it is worthwhile to call to mind the biblical text.

> Abel was a keeper of sheep, but Cain was a tiller of the ground.

And in process of time it came to pass, that Cain brought of the fruit of the ground an offering unto the Lord.

And Abel, he also brought of the firstlings of his flock and of the fat thereof. And the Lord had respect unto Abel and to his offering:

But unto Cain and to his offering he had not respect.

And Cain was very wroth, and his countenance fell.

And the Lord said unto Cain, Why art thou wroth?

And why is thy countenance fallen?

If thou doest well, shalt thou not be accepted? And if thou doest not well, sin lieth at the door. And unto thee shall be his desire, and thou shalt rule over him.

And Cain talked with Abel his brother: and it came to pass, when they were in the field, that Cain rose up against Abel his brother, and slew him.

And the Lord said unto Cain, where is Abel thy brother?

And he said, I know not: am I my brother's keeper?

And he said, What hast thou done? The voice of thy brother's blood crieth unto me from the ground.

And now art thou curst from the earth.

(Genesis 4: 2–11)

In Clough's version, the sacrifices of the brothers are rituals taught by Eve, but disliked by Adam, who regards them as superstitious. Abel is a mother's boy, highly devout, who looks down on his brother and father as unspiritual and godless. He is very conscious of his own standing as one of God's elect:

> *Yea, though I sin, my sin is not to death.*
> *In my repentance I have joy, such joy,*
> *That almost I could sin to seek for it.*

(P: 177)

But he must fight against his sins, and especially against the spiritual pride with which he compares himself with the unelect:

> *Meantime, for that atonement's precious sake*
> *Which in Thy counsels predetermined works*
> *Already to the saving of the saints,*
> *O Father, view with mercy, and forgive;*
> *Nor let my vexed perception of my sin,*
> *Nor any multitude of evil thoughts,*

Crowding like demons in my spirit's house
Nor life, nor death, things here or things below
Cast out the sweet assurance of my soul
That I am Thine, and Thou art mine, my God.

(P: 177)

Cain is riled by his brother's smugness; sometimes he is over-come by ungovernable anger. But more importantly, he feels the need for action, self-initiated action:

to be led
At all, by anyone, and not myself
Is mere dissatisfaction: evermore
Something I must do, individual,
To vindicate my nature, to give proof
I also am, as Adam is, a man.

(P: 178)

The murder of Abel takes place off stage. Adam and Eve hear only a distant cry. When we see Cain alone with Abel's body, his first emotion is surprise; nobody, after all, has ever seen a dead human being before – the first death in the Bible is that of Abel's sacrificial lamb:

What? fallen? so quickly down, so easily felled,
And so completely? Why, he does not move.
Will he not stir – will he not breathe again?
Still as a log, still as his own dead lamb.
Dead is it then? O wonderful! O strange!
Dead! Dead! And can we slay each other then?
If we are wronged, why, we can right ourselves;
If we are plagued and pestered with a fool
That will not let us be, nor leave us room
To do our will and shape our path in peace,
We can be rid of him.

(P: 179)

Cain shouts his jubilation to the distant echo. But then the thought comes: if killing has such permanent effects, ought it not to be more splendid in the enacting?

Yet I could wish that he had struggled more –
That passiveness was disappointing. Ha!

> *He should have writhed and wrestled in my arms,*
> *And all but overcome, and set his knee*
> *Hard on my chest, till I – all faint, yet still*
> *Holding my fingers at his throat – at last,*
> *Inch after inch, had forced him to relax:*
> *But he went down at once, without a word,*
> *Almost without a look.*

(P: 179)

It is after these strenuous verses that Cain hears the voice of a mysterious questioner, which in spite of his rejections will not be silenced.

He takes leave of his mother, asking her to curse him. He rejects her exhortations to repentance and prayer; he seeks not atonement but punishment. It is only when he comes to say goodbye to Adam that he learns for the first time the story of the Fall. The scene is incomplete, and extant in alternative versions. In one Adam tells the story, recommends it should be forgotten:

> *. . . whether a dream, and, if it were a dream,*
> *A transcript of an inward spiritual fact*
> *(As you suggest, and I allow, might be)*
> *Not the less true because it was a dream*
> *I know not*

(P: 182)

In the other version, Adam tries to comfort Cain – not like his mother, by commending repentance, but by speaking of the healing touch of time. But Cain insists that to forget is not to be restored:

> *To lose with time the sense of what we did*
> *Cancels not that we did; what's done remains –*
> *I am my brother's murderer. Woe to me!*
> *Abel is dead. No prayers to empty heaven,*
> *No vegetative kindness of the earth,*
> *Will bring back warmth into his clay again*
> *The gentleness of love into his face.*

(P: 184)

So Cain says goodbye to all thoughts of comfort as delusions:

> *But welcome Fact, and Fact's best brother, Work;*
> *Welcome the conflict of the stubborn soil,*

III

> *To toil the livelong day, and at the end,*
> *Instead of rest, re-carve into my brow*
> *The dire memorial mark of what still is.*
> *Welcome this worship, which I feel is mine;*
> *Welcome this duty –*
> >   *– the solidarity of life*
> *And unity of individual soul.*

(P: 184)

The dramatic impetus of the play comes to an end with Cain's departure into the wilderness. But Clough attempted to round off the drama with a final vision of reconciliation, placed in the mouth of the dying Adam. Reconciliation, indeed, seems to melt mysteriously into cosmic fusion:

> *Abel was gone, and you were gone, my son –*
> *Gone and yet not gone; yea, I seemed to see*
> *The decomposing of those coloured lines*
> *Which we called you, their fusion into one,*
> *And therewithal their vanishing and end.*
> *And Eve said to me 'Adam in the day*
> *When in the inexistent void I heard God's voice,*
> *An awful whisper, bidding me to be,*
> *How sad, how slow to come, how loth to obey*
> *As slow, as sad, as lingeringly loth,*
> *I fade, I vanish, sink and cease to be,*
> *By the same sovereign strong compulsion borne;*
> *Ah, if I vanish, be it into thee!'*
> *She spoke, nor speaking ceased, I listening; but*
> *I was alone – yet not alone – with her*
> *And she with me, and you with us my sons,*
> *As at the first, and yet not wholly – yea,*
> *And that which I had witnessed thus in you,*
> *This fusion and mutation and return,*
> *Seemed in my substance working too.*

Clough was rarely successful in bringing a tortured poem to a serene conclusion. Here, as often elsewhere, the consoling answer proves less convincing than the anguished question.

Both Clough and Hopkins, in their treatment of 'the mighty mythus of the fall' (P: 167) were influenced by Milton's *Paradise Lost*. Both of them recognized Milton as a great master of prosody.

112

They differed, however, in their judgements of him as a man and as a theologian.

Clough wrote in 1839 to J. P. Gell, who was an admirer of Milton's *De Doctrina Christiana*, that he should walk away as fast as he could from Oxford, the seat of orthodoxy:

> It is difficult here even to obtain assent to Milton's greatness as a poet, quite impossible, I should think, if you are unable to say that you 'do not know anything about his prose writings'. Also you must be ready to give up that 'irreverent' third book. Were it not for the happy notion that a man's poetry is not at all affected by his opinions or indeed character and mind altogether, I fear the Paradise Lost would be utterly unsaleable except for waste paper in the University.
>
> (C: 89)

Hopkins had a great admiration for Milton as a poet, and often described his own ideal as 'Miltonic plainness and severity' or as a 'balanced and Miltonic style'. But he rebuked Bridges for writing in praise of Milton as a human being:

> Don't like what you say of Milton, I think he was a very bad man: those who contrary to our Lord's command both break themselves and, as St Paul says, consent to those who break the sacred bond of marriage, like Luther and Milton, fall with eyes open into the terrible judgment of God.
>
> (L, I: 666)

Paradise Lost is concerned not only with the Fall of mankind, but with the sin of the angelic beings which preceded and instigated the temptation of Eve and Adam. Clough, uncomfortable enough with the myth of human Fall, paid little attention to the alleged sin of the angels. But it was a matter which greatly stirred the curiosity of Hopkins, stimulated by the exercises of St Ignatius.

The nature of the angels' sin, he admitted, was a matter most recondite and difficult. None the less, on 14 November 1881 he felt able to report, in his retreat notes, that he had received an increase of light on this mysterious subject:

> The angels, like Adam, were created in sanctifying grace, which is a thing that affects the individual, and were then asked to enter into a covenant or contract with God which,

as with Adam, should give them an original justice or status
and rights before God. The duties of this commonwealth
were, for them, to contribute each in his rank, hierarchy,
and own species, towards the Incarnation and the great
sacrifice.

(S: 200)

To fill out the details of this catastrophe, Hopkins called upon a
Chaldean hieratic text of 600 BC, and a Welsh manuscript of the
fabricator Iolo Morganwg (S: 352–6):

[F]irst I suppose that Christ, in his first stead of angelic
being, led off the angel choir (and in this the Babylonian and
Welsh text agree), calling on all creatures to worship God as
by a kind of *Venite Adoremus*. They obeyed the call, which
indeed was a call into being.

(S: 200)

The effect of this call upon the chief angel, Lucifer, is described thus:

[B]eing required to adore God and enter into a covenant of
justice with him he did so indeed, but, as a chorister who
learns by use in the church itself the strength and beauty of
his voice, he became aware in his very note of adoration of
the riches of his nature; then when from that first note he
should have gone on with the sacrificial service, prolonging
the first note instead and ravished by his own sweetness and
dazzled, the prophet says, by his beauty, he was involved in
spiritual sloth . . . and spiritual luxury and vainglory; to
heighten this, he summoned a train of spirits to be his choir
and, contemptuously breaking with the service of the
eucharistic sacrifice, which was to have a victim of earthly
nature and of flesh, raise a hymn in honour of their own
nature, spiritual purely and ascending, he must have persuaded them, to the divine; and with this sin of pride
aspiring to godhead their crime was consummated.

(S: 179–80)

Hopkins returned, on another occasion, to the comparison
between the primordial cosmic catastrophe and the warbling of a
conceited chorister:

This song of Lucifer's was a dwelling on his own beauty, an
instressing of his own inscape, and like a performance on

the organ and instrument of his own being; it was a sounding, as they say, of his own trumpet and a hymn in his own praise. Moreover, it became an incantation; others were drawn in; it became a concert of voices, a concerting of selfpraise, an enchantment, a magic, by which they were dizzied, dazzled, and bewitched. They would not listen to the note which summoned each to his own place (Jude 6) and distributed them here and there in the liturgy of the sacrifice; they gathered rather closer and closer home under Lucifer's lead and drowned it, raising a countermusic and countertemple and altar, a counterpoint of dissonance and not of harmony. I suppose they introduced a pathos as of a nobler nature put aside for the higher and even persuaded themselves that God was only trying them; that to disobey and substitute themselves Lucifer above all, as the angelic victim of the world sacrifice, was secretly pleasing to him, that selfdevotion to it, the suicide, the semblance of sin was a loveliness of heroism which could only arise in the angelic mind; that it was divine and a meriting and at last a grasp of godhead.

(S: 201)

In this description of the angels' sin Hopkins is going far beyond anything which even the exuberant Roman Catholic theology of the nineteenth century regarded as solidly based in the Scriptures or in the traditional teaching of the Church. That the divine decree foreordaining, in eternity, the incarnation of Christ was prior to the Creation and Fall of angels and of men was a minority opinion of Duns Scotus. Most theologians related the incarnation and redemption to the Fall of Adam. But Hopkins wrote: '[T]he fall was not the reason for Christ's predestination. Even if no angel had fallen, nor any man, Christ would still have been predestined – yes even if no others were to have been created save only Christ' (S: 109).

It was an even more unusual opinion, that the angels fell precisely because they were outraged by the decree that the divine nature should be incarnate in human form. But Hopkins could here appeal to the great Jesuit theologian Suarez. Yet it was totally eccentric to assume that the anger of the rebel angels was focused on a prelapsarian encounter with the body of Christ in its eucharistic manifestation under the form of bread and wine upon the altar. Hopkins tried to support his view with allusions to passages in Scotus; but it has really more in common with the uncanonical, non-scholastic protocols reported by visionaries such as Sister Emmerich and Marie Lataste.

Hopkins was much influenced by both of these mystics to the embarrassment of his Catholic admirers. Christopher Devlin, the admirable Jesuit editor of Hopkins's spiritual writings, drily remarks of Marie Lataste's writings: 'possibly the attribution of long speeches to our Saviour in the first person may tend to diminish rather than increase the confidence of the modern reader' (S: 326). Hopkins's search for Cambrian confirmation of his angelic speculations was not welcomed even by the keenest of Welsh Nationalists. Saunders Lewis remarked, apropos of Iolo Morganwg, that it was sad that Hopkins should so value the rigmarole of an obvious fabrication.

8

SYMBOLS OF GRACE AND GLORY

The place occupied in Clough's poetic sensibility by the Bible was occupied in Hopkins's by the sacramental system. Biographers and critics have made much of the sacramental element in Hopkins's poetry, but the term is often used in very imprecise ways. Sometimes when Hopkins is called a sacramental writer all that is meant is that he takes the beauty of the natural world as a sign of the glory of God. In this sense poems like *God's Grandeur* and *The Starlight Night* are sacramental.

Certainly it is a constant theme of Hopkins's poetry that the appreciation of natural beauty must lead the mind to an awareness of the power and majesty of God. The classic exposition of this theme is the fifth stanza of *The Wreck of the Deutschland*.

> *I kiss my hand*
> *To the stars, lovely-asunder*
> *Starlight, wafting him out of it; and*
> *Glow, glory in thunder;*
> *Kiss my hand to the dappled-with-damson west;*
> *Since, though he is under the world's splendour and wonder*
> *His mystery must be instressed, stressed;*
> *For I greet him the days that I meet him, and bless when I understand.*
>
> (O: 111)

If the world is a creation of God, then the splendour and wonder of the world bear witness to the glory and mystery of God. Just as Aquinas argued, in the fourth of his Five Ways, that the degrees of goodness and being in the world showed that all beings must derive from a single perfect being, so one might seek to argue that the varieties of beauty in the world must be derived from what Clough called a *Summum Pulchrum*.

But this line of thought cannot seriously be called sacramental. The Rocket was not a sacrament of George Stephenson, nor was the *Mona Lisa* a sacrament of Leonardo, though those artefacts bore witness to the ingenuity of the one and the sensibility of the other. A sacrament, in theological precision, is a Christian institution which is an outward sign of inward grace. It must be not just an effect, but a likeness, of the divine reality which it signifies. It belongs in the context not just of creation but of grace; it relates to God not as designer but as redeemer of the world.

There are passages in *The Wreck of the Deutschland* and elsewhere where Hopkins appears to wish to view nature as sacramental in this sense. But it must be confessed that the attempts are perfunctory. Hopkins's incomparable genius for describing nature and natural beauty conceals the fact that the theological linkage between nature and the economy of salvation is often tenuous. This is notoriously so in the case of *The Windhover*, which Hopkins thought, with reason, one of the very best things he had written. The description of the falcon's flight is a marvel of ecstasy, but it is related to religion only by the dedication 'To Christ our Lord'. *Pied Beauty* begins, 'Glory be to God for dappled things', and offers eight packed lines of inscaped nature before concluding, 'He fathers-forth whose beauty is past change:/ Praise him.' The final line reveals, in fact, how *un*like the immutable God is to all that makes the world beautiful.

The sacramentalism of Hopkins is more fruitfully approached if we consider the treatment in his poetry – and also in that of Clough – of the actual sacramental system of the Church. According to Catholic doctrine there are seven, and only seven, sacraments of divine institution: baptism, confirmation, penance, Eucharist, matrimony, order, and the anointing of the sick. These fall into two categories: there are sacraments which are rare and sacraments which are frequent. The rare sacraments are those which are conferred, perhaps only once in a lifetime, to mark particular stages of life or seal the adoption of a particular vocation: baptism, confirmation, matrimony, order, and anointing. The frequent ones are those that form the staple of regular Catholic devotion: penance and Eucharist, that is to say, confession and Communion.

Neither Clough nor Hopkins makes much use of the symbolism of the sacraments of Christian initiation, namely baptism and confirmation. In both poets water imagery, and especially the imagery of rivers and the sea, is omnipresent; but the baptismal imagery, of immersion in water as a symbol of the redeeming death and Resurrection of Jesus, is rarely to be found. Rather perversely, Hopkins uses immersion in water as an image for the sacrament of matrimony. His *Epithalamium* was never completed, but of the fifty-three lines which survive, the first forty-five are a description of boys undressing and bathing in a woodland pond. Only a final couplet relates this scene to the poem's ostensible topic.

> *What is the delightful dean?*
> *Wedlock. What the water? Spousal love.*

(O: 180)

Clough too makes his characters use water imagery to describe matrimony, though in a rather more natural manner. Elspie in *The Bothie* describes the urgency of Philip's wooing as like a salt sea surging into a quiet stream of inland water (P: 81).

As a priest, Hopkins officiated at many marriages. He took a very Pauline view of the relationship to which, at a wedding, husband and wife pledged themselves. In a letter to Patmore, he attacked a writer who said that a wife called her husband lord only by courtesy:

> But he *is* her lord. If it is courtesy only and no consent, then a wife's lowliness is hypocrisy and Christian marriage a comedy, a piece of pretence. . . . And now pernicious doctrines and practice are abroad and the other day the papers said a wretched being refused to say in church the words 'and obey': if it had been a Catholic wedding and I the priest I would have let the sacrilege go no further.

(L: III, 310)

Clough, of course, even while he was an Anglican believer, would not regard matrimony as a sacrament in the Catholic sense. And unlike Hopkins he saw marriage as a union between equal partners. He was not unwilling to see a divine hand in the bringing of spouses together. The conjunction of man, wife, and God in wedlock is beautifully imaged by Elspie in *The Bothie*:

> *it feels to me strangely*
> *Like to the high new bridge, they used to build at, below there*
> *Over the burn and glen on the road. You won't understand me*
> *But I keep saying in my mind – this long time slowly with trouble*
> *I have been building myself up, up, and toilfully raising,*
> *Just like as if the bridge were to do it itself without masons*
> *Painfully getting myself upraised one stone on another,*
> *All one side I mean; and now I see on the other,*
> *Just such another fabric uprising, better and stronger*
> *Close to me, coming to join me: and then I sometimes fancy,*

Sometimes I find myself dreaming at nights about arches and bridges.
Sometimes I dream of a great invisible hand coming down, and
Dropping the great key-stone in the middle: there in my dreaming.
There I feel the great key-stone coming in, and through it
Feel the other part – all the other stones of the archway,
Joined into mine with a strange happy sense of completeness.

(P: 79)

Both Clough and Hopkins were, in their youth, expected by their friends to take orders in the Church of England. For each of them the question of ordination became swallowed up in more fundamental questions: in Clough's case, the impossibility of continued subscription to the thirty-nine articles, and in Hopkins's case his conversion and vocation as a Jesuit. In Clough's poems the priesthood is always treated as a profession rather than as a sacrament; in Hopkins's, the priestly task is naturally seen principally as that of the minister of the other sacraments.

Thus in *The Bugler's First Communion*, Hopkins sees his priestly role as that of dispenser of 'Christ's royal ration' of the Eucharist:

Here he knelt then in regimental red.
Forth Christ from cupboard fetched, how fain I of feet
*   To his youngster take his treat!*
Low-latched in leaf-light housel his too huge godhead.

(O: 147)

And in *Felix Randal* he describes his priestly duty of administering the sacraments of Eucharist and anointing to the dying farrier:

Sickness broke him. Impatient, he cursed at first, but mended
Being anointed and all; though a heavenlier heart began some
Months earlier, since I had our sweet reprieve and ransom
Tendered to him. Ah well, God rest him all road ever he
*   offended.*

(O: 150)

Hopkins valued the sacrament of anointing not only for its spiritual effects; he regarded it as capable also of bringing physical healing. For instance, he wrote to Bridges from Liverpool in 1881:

I have just witnessed a case of remarkable and remarkably rapid recovery from typhus in a little lad whom I anointed. It was no doubt due to the sacrament. His doctor, who gave him up, brought another one today or yesterday to see the phenomenon.

(L, I: 124)

Clough, with his scepticism about miracles, would no doubt have regarded Hopkins's attitude as superstitious. But what most repelled him about the Catholic system was not the idea that the sacraments might have physical effects; it was the idea that they might have spiritual effects. As early as 1838, at a period when he was very attracted by Newman and by a number of the theories of the Tractarians, he wrote: 'I should be very sorry ever to be brought to believe their further views of matter acting on morals as a charm of sacramentalism, and the succession-notion so closely connected with it' (C: 71). This was always Clough's sticking-point in relation to Tractarianism and Catholicism; the theme returns frequently in his diaries and notebooks.

In Hopkins's writings it is above all the sacrament of the Eucharist, and the Real Presence of Christ in the sacrament, which recurs. From his earliest years, Hopkins's devotion to the Eucharist was quite out of the ordinary, even by Roman Catholic standards. Whereas most Catholics believe in the Real Presence because they accept the authority of the Church, Hopkins accepted the authority of the Roman Catholic Church because he believed that nothing less would give him good grounds for believing in the Real Presence. (For this reason his description of his conversion in *The Wreck of the Deutschland* as fleeing 'with a fling of the heart to the heart of the Host' is appropriate, even if dubiously orthodox by strict theological criteria.)

The Eucharist, preserved in the tabernacle on the altar, provided the focus for Hopkins's devotion to Jesus as a person who could be addressed, like a friend, in the privacy of the imagination. His sense of Christ's continuing presence in all the variety of human relationships is something that comes out in many of his verses, and also in sermons and letters.

Thus to Dixon he wrote, apropos of literary fame:

The only just judge, the only just literary critic, is Christ, who prizes, is proud of, and admires, more than any man, more than the receiver himself can, the gifts of his own making. And the only real good which fame and another's praise does is to convey to us, by a channel not at all above suspicion but from circumstances in this case much less to be suspected than the channel of our own minds, some token of the judgment which a perfectly just, heedful, and wise mind, namely Christ's, passes upon our doings.

(L, II: 8)

In a sermon preached at Bedford Leigh he invited the congregation, who had Christ before their eyes masked in the Sacred Host, to think of him as a hero:

> You know how books of tales are written, that put one man before the reader and show him off handsome for the most part and brave and call him My Hero or Our Hero. Often mothers make a hero of a son; girls of a sweetheart and good wives of a husband. Soldiers make a hero of a great general, a party of its leader, a nation of any great man that brings it glory, whether king, warrior, statesman, thinker poet, or whatever it shall be. But Christ, he is the hero.

Christ is the hero of the book of the Gospels. He is a warrior and a conqueror, a king, a statesman, a thinker, an orator, a poet. He is the desire of nations, and all the world's hero; but he is also the hero of single souls:

> He is the true love and the bridegroom of men's souls; the virgins follow him whithersoever he goes; the martyrs follow him through a sea of blood, through great tribulation; all his servants take up their cross and follow him. And those even that do not follow him, yet they look wistfully after him, own him a hero, and wished they dared answer to his call.

No one ever imaged an imaginary friend more full-bloodedly than Hopkins pictured Christ. There met in him, Hopkins said, all things that can make man lovely and lovable. Hopkins felt able to be very specific; early accounts tell us of Jesus that

> he was moderately tall, well built and tender in frame, his features straight and beautiful, his hair inclining to auburn parted in the midst, curling and clustering about the ears and neck as the leaves of a filbert, so they speak, upon the nut. He wore also a forked beard and this as well as the locks upon his head were never touched by razor or shears; neither, his health being perfect, could a hair ever fall to the ground.

(S: 34–5)

'I make no secret,' he concluded, 'I look forward with eager desire to seeing the matchless beauty of Christ's body in the heavenly light.' But higher than this beauty of body was the beauty of Christ's mind, his genius and wisdom; and higher than all of this the beauty of his character, full of grace and truth (S: 38).

While the Eucharist, and the presence of Christ in the host on the altar, is a topic which recurs over and over in Hopkins's poetry, there is very little reference to the other frequent Christian sacrament, the sacrament of penance. Perhaps he felt it would be improper, a violation of the seal of the confessional, to make any poetic use, even in the most general terms, of his experience as a priest listening to the sins of penitents.

There have been preserved the records of Hopkins's own examinations of conscience in preparation for confession in his Anglican days. They bear a resemblance to the records of sins in Clough's undergraduate diaries, prepared not for confession but for self-reproach. In his later life, at least, Clough seems to have felt that the Christian doctrine of repentance and atonement involved some incoherent attempt to undo the past or at least blot it from the mind. Such, at least, are the sentiments which he puts into the mouth of Cain, when Eve, after the murder of Abel, urges him to seek atonement from a gracious God, and to prostrate his soul in penitential prayer:

> *I ask not for atonement, mother mine;*
> *I ask but one thing – never to forget.*
> *I ask but – not to add to one great crime*
> *Another self-delusion scarcely less.*

> (P: 181)

Clough's fullest treatment of the Catholic sacrament of penance – one which indeed gives voice to his distrust of the whole sacramental system – is a poem written between 1849–50, but first published in 1951, entitled *Sa Majesté très Chrétienne*. In its final form the poem consists entirely of an address by Louis XV to his father confessor. In an earlier version this was preceded by a scene in which the king fondles his mistresses ('Would I had mouths as berries on a bush/ for all of you at once to pick in kisses') which contains the lines:

> *We will all go you know at last to heaven,*
> *Confess our naughty deeds, repent, receive*
> *The wafer and the unction of the Church*

And so – through Purgatory pass to heaven:
And Purgatory also is not long,
But much like penance upon Earth; ye say
The seven penitential psalms, repeat
Eight or nine prayers with holy meditations
And so, washed white, and clad in virgin robes
The good kind God receives us to himself.
You laugh, my pet ones. Ah I mean it though,
Yes, and tomorrow, I will not forget;
I'll bring with me the Catechism of Trent
And test you in your faiths, my little ones.

(P: 671)

In Clough's final fair copy, printed in *Poems*, the poem begins instead in the tone of self-pitying self-justification which is the keynote of the whole:

'Tis true, Monseigneur, I am much to blame;
But we must all forgive; especially
Subjects their King; would I were one to do so
What could I do? and how was I to help it?
'Tis true it should not be so: true indeed,
I know I am not what I would I were.
I would I were, as God intended me,
A little quiet harmless acolyte
Clothed in long serge and linen shoulder-piece
Day after day
To pace serenely through the sacred fane,
Bearing the sacred things before the priest,
Curtsey before that altar as we pass,
And place our burden reverently on this.
There – by his side to stand and minister,
To swing the censer and to sound the bell,
Uphold the book, the patin change and cup –
Ah me –
And why does childhood ever change to man?

(P: 195)

Only the sacraments make adult life tolerable:

Ah, holy father, yes.
Without the appointed,
Without the sweet confessional relief,

> *Without the welcome, all-absolving words,*
> *The mystic rite, the solemn soothing forms,*
> *Our human life were miserable indeed.*
>
> (P: 196)

For kings, life is especially difficult, even with the sacraments:

> *And yet methinks our holy Mother Church*
> *Deals hardly, very, with her eldest born,*
> *Her chosen, sacred, and most Christian Kings.*
> *To younger pets, the blind, the halt, the sick,*
> *The outcast child, the sinners of the street*
> *Her doors are open and her precinct free;*
> *The beggar finds a nest, the slave a home,*
> *Even thy altars, O my Mother Church –*
> *O templa quam dilecta. We, the while,*
> *Poor Kings, must forth to action, as you say,*
> *Action, that slaves us, drives us, fretted, worn,*
> *To pleasure, which anon enslaves us too;*
> *Action, and what is Action, O my God?*

The world is a perplexing labyrinth. Can anyone say that one path rather than another leads to God? Can anything a puny human hand can enact conduce in any way to the glory of God from all eternity? The confessor reminds the King of the commandments, and of the teaching of the Scriptures and the Church; a voice is with us ever at our ear:

> *Yes, holy Father, I am thankful for it;*
> *Most thankful I am not, as other men,*
> *A lonely Lutheran English Heretic;*
> *If I had so by God's despite been born,*
> *Alas, methinks I had but passed my life*
> *In sitting motionless beside the fire,*
> *Not daring to remove the once-placed chair*
> *Nor stir my foot for fear it should be sin.*
> *Thank God indeed,*
> *Thank God for his infallible certain creed.*
>
> (P: 197)

But for kings the commandments are not easy to read, and 'Ministers somehow have small faith in them'. It must be much easier to be a priest and religious – or at least a lay brother:

Would I were out in quiet Paraguay
Mending the Jesuits' shoes!

(P: 198)

The monarch concludes his confession not so much by repenting his sins as by disowning them:

No satisfaction find I any more
In the old pleasant evil ways; but less,
Less, I believe, of those uneasy stirs
Of discontented and rebellious will
That once with self-contempt tormented me.
Depraved, that is, degraded am I – Sins
Which yet I see not how I should have shunned,
Have, in despite of all the means of grace,
Submission perfect to the appointed creed,
And absolution-plenary and prayers,
Possessed me, held, and changed – yet after all
Somehow I think my heart within is pure.

(P: 198)

By placing that final desperate whimper of self-delusion in the mouth of the kneeling Louis XV, the poet clinches his message that the sacramental system is powerless to prevent sin and productive only of an illusion of righteousness.

9

THE KINGDOM OF THIS WORLD

Neither Clough nor Hopkins in the early phases of their religious development seem to have been led by their religious principles into any involvement with social and political questions. Both held a highly introspective concept of spiritual development, and both placed a high religious value on withdrawal from the world.

It was during Clough's years at Oriel that he turned from being an apolitical student into someone with a reputation as a radical social reformer. But already, as an undergraduate, he showed one concern which linked his early unworldliness with his later radicalism. His diaries show that he resented the weight placed by many of his contemporaries on a code of manners, and he became disillusioned with the ideal of gentlemanliness held up by the class to which he belonged. An early entry describes as very necessary 'the annihilation and extirpation of all my false shame and miserable approbativeness and degraded dependency *in rebus gentlemanlicis*'. A speech of Clough's at a Balliol debating society was long remembered, in which he defended the motion 'that the character of a gentleman was in the present day made too much of' (PPR, 1: 26).

It is interesting to contrast Clough's lifelong dislike of the very concept of 'gentleman' with Hopkins's attitude to gentlemanliness. While admitting that 'to be a gentleman is but on the brim of morals and rather a thing of manners than of morals properly', Hopkins went so far, in a letter to Bridges in 1883, as to compare the quality of gentlemanliness with the humility which St Paul extolled in Christ. A true gentleman was in a position to despise the greatest poet or painter for anything which showed him not to be a gentleman:

> The quality of a gentleman is so very fine a thing that it seems to me one should not be at all hasty in concluding that one possesses it. . . . And the more a man feels what it means and is – and to feel this is certainly some part of it – the more backward he will be to think he can have realised in

himself anything so perfect. It is true, there is nothing like the truth and 'the good that does not know itself scarce is'; so the perfect gentlemen will know that he is the perfect gentleman. But few can be in a position to know this and, being imperfect gentlemen, it will perhaps be a point of their gentlemanliness, for a gentleman is modest, to feel that they are not perfect gentlemen.

By the by if the English race had done nothing else, yet if they left the world the notion of a gentleman, they would have done a great service to mankind.

(L, I: 175)

Clough admired, and indeed practised, the virtues such as modesty which Hopkins saw as characteristic of the gentleman. But he became more and more aware of the social price to be paid by the many if some few were to be in a position to exhibit gentlemanly refinements. During his Oriel years, from 1844, he worked as a volunteer at the offices of the Oxford Mendicity Society in the slums of St Ebbe's, distributing meal-tickets and helping to administer a hostel and soup-kitchen. His consciousness of the social cost of Victorian civilization was sharpened, during his Oriel years, by the terrible famine which broke out in 1847 in Ireland.

The effects of the famine were worsened by the prevalent *laissez-faire* economic doctrines according to which any attempt to provide relief for those in want would, in the long term, increase the gravity of the situation. But at Oxford a group concerned by the sufferings of the Irish formed a Retrenchment Association with the object of inducing members of the university to at least restrain their unnecessary expenditure during the period of distress. Clough joined the association and helped to propagate its aims. His first substantial publication was a pamphlet in its support:

> God, by a sudden visitation, has withdrawn from the income He yearly sends us in the fruits of his earth, sixteen millions sterling. Withdrawn it, and from whom? On whom falls the loss? Not on the rich and luxurious, but on those whose labour makes the rich man rich and gives the luxurious his luxury. Shall not we, then, the affluent and indulgent, spare somewhat of our affluence, curtail somewhat of our indulgence, that these (for our wealth too and our indulgence in the end) may have food while they work, and have work to gain them food. . . .
>
> Let not the sky which in Ireland looks upon famishment

and fever see us here in Oxford in the midst of health and strength and over-eating, overdrinking, and over-enjoying. Let us not scoff at eternal justice with our champagne and our claret, our breakfasts and suppers, our club dinners and desserts, wasteful even to the worst taste, luxurious even to unwholesomeness, – or yet again by our silly and fantastic frippery or dandyism in the hazardous elaboration of which the hundred who fail are sneered at, and the one who succeeds is smiled at.

(PPR, 1: 275, 279)

Clough rehearses undergraduate objections to cutting down their spending and giving alms. They have no money of their own; it is all their parents'. To cut down on expenditure would take the bread out of the mouths of Oxford tradesmen and their workpeople. If saving is possible at all, debts must be paid before alms are given. Or perhaps, simplest and boldest: 'The money is mine, and I will have the good of it; I have got it, and I will spend; the Irish have not, and they must do without.'

Clough answers each of the objections in turn:

The sum which last year the paternal purse would have freely given for ices, will it this year refuse for almsgiving? . . . Do not, in the name of common sense, first refuse to give, because the money is not yours, and then go and spend it on yourself, because it is your father's.

(PPR, 1: 274)

Most true it is that the indulgences of Members of this University are the means of providing a livelihood for a large staff of shopkeepers and shopkeepers' work-people, tailors and confectioners, ostlers and waiters. Most true it is. Yet except for the mere enjoyment so received by us, the customers, our money is a mere waste. We are employing for our enjoyments, men who might by devoting their skill and their strength to the farm, the factory, the ship and the railway, increase our stock of food, and our facilities for obtaining and transmitting it. . . . Surely it is idle to keep up an unnatural and vicious demand which finds no better way of feeding one set of men than wasting food on another.

(PPR, 1: 276)

It is to be feared that there are some, who with money in their pockets will refuse to give to the Irish, because they owe sums to tradesmen; neglect to pay their tradesmen because paying tradesmen is not giving to Ireland; and so in the end will do neither. . . . Pay your debts by all means: I ask you not to be generous before you are just; I only bid you make haste and be just that you may be generous the sooner.

(PPR, 1: 278–9)

But was giving to the starving a matter of generosity rather than justice? The argument from private property was a two-edged matter: beware of asking, 'May I not do what I like with my own?' Every man's wealth came from his own or his ancestors' work, and ultimately from the earth which forms our real wealth and subsistence. And, according to Scripture, 'the earth hath He given to the children of men' – not to the children of the rich, or of the noble, or of those who have had it hitherto:

So far as without encouraging present idleness and improvidence, without encroaching unduly on provisions for posterity, it were possible to equalise the distribution of labour, so far were that equalisation a duty. . . .

Let it be fairly felt that what we call bounty and charity is not, as we fain would persuade ourselves, a matter of gratuitous uncalled-for condescension – as of God to men, or men to meaner animals, as of children feeding the robins or ladies watering their flowers, but on the contrary a supplementary but integral part of fair dealing; the payment of a debt of honour. . . . As a matter of pure justice and not of generosity, England is bound to share her last crust with Ireland, and the rich men to fare as the poor.

(PPR, 1: 282–3)

Some would argue that there are things worse than starving, and things better than eating and drinking. Society has higher objects than preserving the lives of individuals; we have inherited a great civilization, and just as ignorant parents stint themselves to provide education for their children, so the laborious poor of the land support, at their painful cost, the aristocracy of the rich and civilized.

Clough is prepared to agree that if there is any justification for inequalities between ranks it must be based on the possibility which such inequalities allow for refinement and civilization. But that is a very different thing from setting up the luxury and ostentation of some as justification for the poverty and degradation of others. In showing how the rich pass from one argument to the other, Clough falls into spluttering Carlylean rage:

> To what result do we come? To something like this. First of all, that the welfare of the nation does undoubtedly require the existence of a class free for the most part to follow their own devices; that it is right that there should be men with time at their disposal and money in their purses, and large liberty in public opinion; men who though thousands and tens of thousands perish by starvation, stoically meanwhile in books and in study, reading, and thinking, and travelling, and – it would seem too, enjoying, in hunting, videlicet, and shooting, in duets, and dancing, by ball-going and grousing, by dejeuners and deer-stalking, by foie-gras and johannisberger, by February strawberries and December green peas, by turbot and turtle, and venison, should pioneer the route of the armies of mankind; should, an intrepid forlorn hope, lead the way up the breach of human destiny to the citadel of truth.
>
> (PPR, I: 284)

> No such thing can there be as a right to do what you will with your own. The property is not your own: scarcely your own at any time; during times of calamity in no wise, except to do good with and distribute. Neither again can you plead the good it does you: who made thee to differ? You cannot even plead the good which your cultivation, so obtained, does the nation.
>
> (PPR, I: 286)

It was no doubt in part due to the Retrenchment pamphlet that Clough acquired a reputation as a radical. This increased after his time in Paris during the 1848 Revolution, and in July of that year he told Thomas Arnold that he was regarded as the wildest and most *écervelé* republican in Oxford. When *The Bothie* appeared, among the epithets applied to it in Oxford, he told Emerson (C, 1: 240), were 'immoral and Communistic'.

On the topic of private property Hopkins wrote nothing comparable to the Retrenchment pamphlet. As a Jesuit, he gave up all property of his own, by his vow of poverty; but in itself that no more meant that property was theft than his vow of chastity meant that marriage was adultery. But he was at one time not unwilling to speak in favour of communism.

In a letter to Bridges in August 1871 he said that he was 'always thinking of the Communist future'. Like Clough, he thought that Carlyle had been ahead of his time. Speaking of the social disorders of the time, he said:

> It is what Carlyle has long threatened and foretold. But his writings are, as he might himself say, 'most inefficacious-strenuous heaven-protestations, caterwaul, and Cassandra-wailings . . .'
>
> However, I am afraid some great revolution is not far off. Horrible to say, in a manner I am a Communist. Their ideal bating some things is nobler than that professed by any secular statesman I know of (I must own that I live in bat-light and shoot at a venture). Besides it is just. – I do not mean that the means of getting to it are. But it is a dreadful thing for the greatest and most necessary part of a very rich nation to live a hard life without dignity, knowledge, comforts, delight, or hopes in the midst of plenty – which plenty they make. . . .
>
> England has grown hugely wealthy but the wealth has not reached the working classes; I expect it has made their condition worse. Besides this iniquitous order the old civilization embodies another order mostly old and what is new in direct entail from the old, the old religion, learning, law, art, etc. and all the history that is preserved in standing monuments. But as the working classes have not been educated they know next to nothing of all this and cannot be expected to care if they destroy it.
>
> (L, I: 27–8)

Hopkins's partial endorsement of Communism is more surprising than Clough's 'Communistic' remarks in the 'hungry forties'; not only because Hopkins's politics were in general much more conservative than Clough's, but because in the year Hopkins's letter was written the history of the Paris Commune had shown the brutal, as well as the heroic, aspect of communism. Hopkins was well aware of this; as he said in his next letter: 'I have little reason to be red: it was the red Commune that murdered five of our Fathers lately.'

If Hopkins wrote less political prose than Clough, his concern for the desperate condition of the working class found its way into his poetry much more than a similar concern ever did with Clough. This was due to his experience as a curate in some of the most depressing city slums, especially in Liverpool in the church of St Francis Xavier.

Before this his distaste for the 'sordid, turbid, time' of Victorian capitalism seems not so much social compassion as romantic disdain. Thus, in *God's Grandeur* he writes:

> Generations have trod, have trod, have trod;
>   And all is seared with trade; bleared, smeared with toil;
> And wears man's smudge and shares man's smell: the soil
>   Is bare now, nor can foot feel, being shod.
>
> (O: 128)

The tone has quite changed by the time of *Tom's Garland*, written in the last year of his life. The poem begins with a description of navvies knocking off work and piling their picks, striking sparks with their hobnails as they set off home. By now Hopkins is well aware of the advantages of good footwear:

> Tom – garlanded with squat and surly steel
> Tom; then Tom's fallowbootfellow piles pick
> By him and rips out rockfire homeforth – sturdy Dick;
> Tom Heart-at-Ease, Tom Navvy: he is all for his meal
> Sure's bed now.

The labourer's lot is low, but it is carefree; why then should we worry about the divisions in society? The poem continues:

> Commonweal
> Little I reck ho! lacklevel in, if all had bread:
> What! Country is honour enough in all us – lordly head,
> With heaven's lights high hung round, or, mother-ground
> That mammocks, mighty foot. But no way sped,
> Nor mind nor mainstrength, gold go garlanded
> With, perilous, O no; nor yet plod safe shod sound;
>   Undenizened, beyond bound
> Of earth's glory, earth's ease, all; no-one nowhere
> In wide the world's weal; rare gold, bold steel, bare
>   In both; care, but share care –
> This, by Despair, bred Hangdog dull; by Rage,
> Manwolf, worse; and their packs infest the age.
>
> (O: 178)

These lines are not only some of the most intense that Hopkins wrote but also some of the most difficult, and we are fortunate to possess an account of the poem's meaning written for Bridges very soon after its composition. The meaning, Hopkins says is this:

> [T]he commonwealth or well ordered human society is like one man; a body with many members and each its function; some higher, some lower, but all honourable, from the honour which belongs to the whole. The head is the sovereign, who has no superior but God . . . covered, so to say, only with the sun and stars, of which the crown is a symbol. . . . The foot is the daylabourer, and this is armed with hobnail boots, because it has to wear and be worn by the ground; which again is symbolical; for it is navvies or daylabourers who, on the great scale or in gangs and millions, mainly trench, tunnel, blast, and in other ways disfigure, 'mammock' the earth and, on a small scale, singly and superficially, stamp it with their footprints. And the 'garlands' of nails they wear are therefore the visible badge of the place they fill, the lowest in the commonwealth. But this place still shares the common honour, and if it wants one advantage, glory or public fame, makes up for it by another, ease of mind, absence of care; and these things are symbolised by the gold and iron garlands. . . .
>
> The witnessing of which lightheartedness makes me indignant with the fools of Radical Levellers. But presently I remember that this is all very well for those who are in, however, low in, the Commonwealth and share in any way the Common weal; but that the curse of our times is that many do not share it, that they are outcasts from it and have neither security nor splendour; that they share care with the high and obscurity with the low, but wealth or comfort with neither.

But Hopkins's compassion with the unemployed no longer turned his thoughts towards communism or socialism. On the contrary, this moving exegesis concludes with the sentence: 'And this state of things, I say, is the origin of Loafers, Tramps, Cornerboys, Roughs, Socialists and other pests of society' (L, I: 273).

For the greater part of Hopkins's life his dominant political emotion was patriotism. Even the writing of poetry he saw as a patriotic duty:

A great work by an Englishman is like a great battle won by England. It is an unfading bay tree. It will even be admired by and praised by and do good to those who hate England (as England is most perilously hated), who do not wish even to be benefited by her.

(L, I: 231)

As an instance of a poetic work which brought glory to England he cited, on another occasion, Wordsworth's Immortality Ode: 'For my part I should think St George and St Thomas of Canterbury wore roses in heaven for England's sake on the day that ode, not without their intercession, was penned' (L, II: 148).

Since he regarded patriotism as a virtue that would survive even into heaven, it is not surprising that Hopkins set a very high value on military valour. 'Why do we all, seeing of a soldier, bless him? bless/ Our redcoats, our tars?' he asked in a sonnet of 1885. After all, most soldiers and sailors are frail creatures at best. It is the nobility of the calling, Hopkins says, which makes us admire the men;

> the heart
> *Since, proud, it calls the calling manly, gives a guess*
> *That, hopes that, makesbelieve the men must be no less.*

(O: 168)

When Hopkins sent the manuscript of *The Bugler's First Communion* to Bridges, he wrote: 'I am half inclined to hope the Hero of it may be killed in Afghanistan.' Nothing disgusted him more than military cowardice. During the war in the Transvaal he wrote to Bridges (1 May 1881): 'We have been shamefully beaten by the Boers (at Majuba it was simply that our troops funked and ran), but this is not the worst that is to be' (L, I: 128). He returned to the theme a month later:

> The state of the country is indeed sad, I might say it is heart-breaking, for I am a very great patriot. Lamentable as the condition of Ireland is, there is hope of things mending, but the Transvaal is an unredeemed disgrace. And people do not seem to mind. You know that our troops ('our gallant fellows', as the reporter had it) ran.

(L, I: 132)

At no point does he make any inquiry into the justice of the causes for which British troops were sent to the Transvaal or to

Afghanistan. The efficiency of British military operations may be criticized, but their justification remains unquestioned.

It was Hopkins's keenly English patriotism which was one of the factors that made him so unhappy during his last years in Ireland. In his letters he mentions the pain he feels at the hostility to England to be met with in Dublin. It is almost unheard of for Hopkins, in his letters, to criticize Catholic authorities; but when it comes to the Irish nationalist bishops he minces no words, even to the non-Catholic Bridges:

> Yesterday Archbishop Walsh had a letter in the *Freeman* enclosing a subscription to the defence of Dillon and the other traversers on trial for preaching the Plan of Campaign and saying that the jury was packed and a fair trial impossible. The latter was his contribution to the cause of concord and civil order. Today Archbishop Croke has one proposing to pay no taxes. One archbishop backs robbery, the other rebellion; the people in good faith believe and will follow them. You see it is the beginning of the end: Home Rule or separation is near. Let them come: anything is better than the attempt to rule a people who own no principle of civil obedience at all, not only to the existing government but to none at all. I should be glad to see Ireland happy, even though it involved the fall of England, if that could come about without shame or guilt. But Ireland will not be happy: a people without a principle of allegiance cannot be; moreover this movement has throughout been promoted by crime.
>
> (L, I: 252)

In his retreat notes at the beginning of his last year of life, Hopkins reveals that he feels himself involved in the crimes of Irish nationalism, through the salary he earns for the Irish Jesuits:

> [T]he Catholic Church in Ireland and the Irish Province in it and our College in that are greatly given over to a partly unlawful cause, promoted by partly unlawful means, and against my will my pains, laborious and distasteful, like prisoners made to serve the enemies gunners, go to help on this cause.
>
> (S: 262)

A few months before, Hopkins had written to Bridges: 'I had in my mind the first verse of a patriotic song for soldiers, the words I mean: heaven knows it is needed.' The finished version runs:

> *What shall I do for the land that bred me,*
> *Here homes and fields that folded and fed me?*
> *Be under her banner and live for her honour:*
> *Under her banner I'll live for her honour.*
>   Chorus: *Under her banner we live for her honour.*
>
> *Not the pleasure, the pay, the plunder,*
> *But country and flag, the flag I am under –*
> There *is the shilling that finds me willing*
> *To follow a banner and fight for honour.*
>   Ch.: *We follow her banner, we fight for her honour.*
>
> *Call me England's fame's fond lover*
> *Her fame to keep, her fame to recover.*
> *Spend me or end me what God shall send me,*
> *But under her banner I live for her honour.*
>   Ch.: *Under her banner we march for her honour.*
>
> *Where is the field I must play the man on?*
> *O welcome there their steel or cannon.*
> *Immortal beauty is death with duty*
> *If under her banner I fall for her honour.*
>   Ch.: *Under her banner we fall for her honour.*
>
>   (O: 181–2)

When he wrote that, Hopkins had less than a year to live. Fortunately, he was able to compose four more poems, including the magnificent *To R.B.* It would have been very sad if the final stanza of that song had been the last specimen of his talent.

10

THE DRAMA OF DIPSYCHUS

The long poetic dialogue *Dipsychus* contains some of Clough's finest verse. Had he ever brought it into final shape it would no doubt count as his masterpiece; certainly it would rank with *The Bothie* and with *Amours de Voyage*. However, though he thoroughly revised the poem at least thrice after writing the first draft in Venice in 1850, he never brought it into a form which satisfied him. His wife, to whom it fell to prepare his unpublished poems for post-humous publication, was faced with a difficult editorial problem, made more severe by her distaste for parts of the poem which she regarded as licentious or irreligious. In the first posthumous edition of the poems several sections of the work were printed as separate poems. Some of these may indeed have originally been conceived as such by Clough himself and only later incorporated into the dialogue. Others he may have wished to publish separately, having despaired of completing the entire poem. The work was printed privately as a unit in 1865 and published generally in 1869. In recent times fuller versions have been printed, reproducing more of the material to be found in the manuscripts, including some which had been rejected by Clough in later revisions. The fullest version is that of 1974, which includes material which even in the 1951 edition appears only in an appendix.

It would be wrong to think, however, that the 1974 editor printed the full text of a poem which had been given in mutilated form by previous editors. Given Clough's changes of mind, and ultimate indecision, there is no such thing as *the* text of the poem. The situation is similar to that of some of Verdi's operas, such as *Don Carlos*, where several quite differently structured scores can make an equal claim to authenticity. It may well be that the long version of the poem published in *Poems*, with its parallel passages and repetitions, contains material which Clough regarded as alternative rather than consecutive passages for the final version as he envisaged it.

In all its versions the poem is a dialogue, set in Venice. In some versions the work is topped and tailed by a prologue and epilogue in prose, in the form of a conversation between the poet and his uncle. In the prose epilogue, at one point, the poet describes its theme as 'the conflict between the tender conscience and the world'. The two characters are named, in the earliest versions, Faustulus and Mephisto; later, these names were altered to Dipsychus and the Spirit, and Clough began to use the title *Dipsychus* for the whole poem.

The Greek word *dipsychus* is one which does not occur in classical Greek, but is used in the New Testament in the Epistle of St James. It occurs twice, at 1: 8 in a verse translated in the Authorized Version 'A double minded man is unstable in all his ways', and at 4: 8: 'Cleanse your hands, ye sinners; and purify your hearts, ye double minded.' Clough copied these passages in Greek into his early diaries; and when as an undergraduate he wished to describe the evil state of his soul it was often the Greek word *dipsychus* which he used.

But we do not need arcane external evidence to show that the Dipsychus of the poem is to be identified, in some manner, with the poet himself. The first scene, set in the piazza at Venice on a Sunday evening, begins with a speech by Dipsychus:

> *The scene is different, and the place: the air*
> *Tastes of the nearer North: the people too*
> *Not perfect southern lightness. Wherefore then*
> *Should those old verses come into my mind*
> *I made last year at Naples?*

> (P: 218)

Dipsychus then quotes at some length from *Easter Day*, interrupted by ironic *sotto voce* asides from the Spirit. Clearly we are invited to identify the character in the dialogue with the poet of *Easter Day*. Dipsychus is not a fully fictional character like the Claude of *Amours de Voyage* – though later in the poem he will quote verses of Claude's as his own without acknowledgement. (Compare *Dipsychus*, 5: 72, which echoes *Amours*, III: 173, 1: 'All as I go on my way, I behold them consorting and coupling/ Faithful it seemeth and fond, very fond, very probably faithful.')

What of the other character in the dialogue? Are we to identify him with the Devil, as the earlier name Mephisto suggests? Or are we to regard the two characters as two halves of the two-souled man? Identification with the Devil would be rash, even though in the final scene, even in later versions, Dipsychus addresses the Spirit as Mephisto. When Clough altered the names Mephisto and

Faustulus, he was not simply removing an invitation to comparison with Goethe, though he may indeed have come to think such an invitation impudent. The development of the poem itself made it important that the nature of Dipsychus's interlocutor should remain ambiguous. It would be equally wrong, on the other hand, to think that the divisions within the two-souled man are represented exhaustively by the two characters. The character Dipsychus himself is torn in more than one direction by his encounter with the Spirit. (In scene 11 he exclaims: 'O double self! And I untrue to both.')

In fact, at both the beginning and the end of the poem, we are made aware of the Spirit's ambiguous nature. Dipsychus asks, at the beginning of the second scene:

> *What is this persecuting voice that haunts me?*
> *What? Whence? of whom? How am I to detect?*
> *Myself or not myself? My own bad thoughts,*
> *Or some external agency at work*
> *To lead me who knows whither?*

(P: 222)

In the final prose epilogue the ambiguity is taken further; it is in doubt not only whether the Spirit is internal or external, but also whether or not he is genuinely evil. The poet explains to his uncle:

> Perhaps he wasn't a devil after all. That's the beauty of the poem; nobody can say. You see, dear sir, the thing which it is attempted to represent is the conflict between the tender conscience and the world. Now, the over-tender conscience will, of course, exaggerate the wickedness of the world; and the Spirit in my poem may be merely the hypothesis or subjective imagination.

The Spirit himself in the twelfth scene says:

> *The Devil oft the Holy Scripture uses*
> *But God can act the Devil when he chooses.*

(P: 281)

When, in the final scene, the Spirit accepts for himself a number of biblical names for diabolical powers ('I've got a score/ never a royal baby more/ for a brass plate upon a door') – especially 'The Power of this World' as denounced by St Paul in the Ephesians – we

which it is the centrepiece is not as clear as it would be if it really matched the title which Mrs Clough gave it when she published it separately: *Spectator ab extra*.

In *Amours de Voyage*, Claude expressed his distaste for much of the ecclesiastical architecture of Rome. It did not fit his ideal of Christianity, with its 'exaltations sublime, and yet diviner abasements':

> *No, the Christian faith, as I, at least understood it,*
> *Is not here, O Rome, in any of these thy churches;*
> *Is not here, but in Freiburg, or Rheims, or Westminster Abbey.*
> *What in thy Dome I find, in all thy recent efforts,*
> *Is a something, I think, more rational far, more earthly*
> *Actual, less ideal, devout not in scorn and refusal,*
> *But in a positive, calm, Stoic-Epicurean acceptance.*

> (P: 96)

The Spirit makes a similar judgement about the relation between Gothic and classical architecture; but he is drawn rather to the classical. As the trip up the Grand Canal nears its end, he commends 'the shapely Grecian column' and 'Palladio's pediments and bases':

> *Maturer optics don't delight*
> *In childish dim religious light*
> *In evanescent vague effects*
> *That shirk, not face, one's intellects;*
> *They love not fancies fast betrayed,*
> *And artful tricks of light and shade,*
> *But pure form nakedly displayed*
> *And all things absolutely made.*

> (P: 244)

As the scene comes to its close, the theme of appearance and reality, truth and illusion, begins to dominate the verse. Dipsychus revels in the deceptive light effects of the rising moon, the glorious and portentous reflections of the historic buildings in the waters of the canal. The Spirit is contemptuous of 'these airy blisses, skiey joys':

> *The shadows lie, the glories fall,*
> *And are but moonshine after all.*

> (P: 245)

At sunset it is futile to look, with Wordsworth, for

> *something far more deeply interfused,*
> *Whose dwelling is the light of setting suns,*
> *And the round ocean and the living air,*
> *And the blue sky, and in the mind of man:*
> *A motion and a spirit, that impels*
> *All thinking things, the objects of all thought,*
> *And rolls through all things.*

No – once the gondolier has been paid off, the thing to do is to try an ice:

> *Let me induce you to join me*
> *In* gramolata persici . . .

13

BO PEEP'S LOST SHEEP

The part of *Dipsychus* which runs from scene 9 to scene 14 could be entitled 'The Submission of Dipsychus'. In the first part Dipsychus rejected, after whatever hesitation, the suggestions of the tempting Spirit. In the entr'acte he affirmed, in a series of lyrics quoted from the poet's past, the independence of the self from the world and from others. Now in this final section, reluctantly but inevitably, he comes to terms with the world which speaks through the Spirit.

The resolution of the first part of the poem was imperfect. The religious problem was not solved, but smothered under momentary high spirits. Christ might be risen on the Lido, but what of the rest of life when the holiday in Venice comes to its end? The passenger in life's gondola can proclaim his spiritual independence of the world only provided he can rely on financial independence in the world, as the Spirit underlines in his vulgar, topper-and-cane, music-hall lyric. In these final scenes Dipsychus looks his own mundane future in the face; he will have to earn his living, and do so on the world's terms. Venice henceforth appears only as a symbol of the life to which he is saying goodbye.

That symbolism is first used in the lyric about the Academy exhibition which prefaces the final sequence of scenes. Two paintings, one of Byron in Greece, one of the Virgin assumed into heaven, stand beside each other. One stands for the life of action and the other for the life of contemplation. The poet, in the lyric, opts for the life of action, rejecting the pursuit of pleasure, fame, profit, or artistry in word or paint:

> *If live we positively must*
> *God's name be blest for noble deeds . . .*

(P: 264)

The 'submission of Dipsychus' starts with Dipsychus imagining himself performing some historic action comparable to Byron's liberation of Greece. But the imagination is punctured almost as soon as it is given shape. For if Byron, in the Academy, symbolizes noble deeds, a moment ago on the Lido he was the icon of unthinking animal spirits. The Assumption of the Virgin may be the beatification of the contemplative; but it was the Feast of the Assumption, a few scenes back, which provided the scenario for the street-walkers. The poet's own verse becomes a symbol for the illusions that must be given up:

> *Verses! well, they are made, so let them go*
> *No more if I can help. This is one way*
> *The procreant heat and fervour of our youth*
> *Escapes, in puff, and smoke, and shapeless words*
> *Of mere ejaculation, nothing worth,*
> *Unless to make maturer years content*
> *To slave in base compliance to the world.*

(P: 265)

Hopkins, when he became a Jesuit, burned his verses because he felt they would interfere with his new vocation. They were part of the world on which he was turning his back. Dipsychus on the contrary gives up his verses as part of coming to terms with the world. The renunciation was carried out, both symbolically in the poem, and in reality in the poet's life. In the rest of the poem, though Dipsychus utters some of Clough's finest blank verse, there is no – with one significant exception – further lyric comparable to those of the entr'acte. And after *Dipsychus* was laid aside and Clough turned his attention to marriage and career, he produced almost no verse to match the standard of his golden years of 1848–50.

Dipsychus's resolve to give up verse antedates the opening of his negotiations with Mephistopheles. These begin, on Dipsychus's side, with some characteristic hedging:

> *Should I conceive (not that at all I do,*
> *'Tis curiosity that prompts my speech) –*
> *A wish to bargain for your merchandise,*
> *Say what were your demands? What were your terms?*
> *What should I do? What should I cease to do?*
> *What incense on what altars must I burn?*
> *And what abandon? What unlearn, or learn?*
> *Religion goes, I take it.*

(P: 266)

Dipsychus should have known better after overhearing the Spirit's remarks in part one. So far from religion being an obstacle to sincere worldliness, the Church provides one of the most desirable professions for someone like Dipsychus – though he should avoid devoutness, which is merely vague emotion, and theology, which merely provides matter for litigation in the ecclesiastical courts. But if Dipsychus should prefer a legal career, Mephistopheles will offer his help and influence. Moreover, he will find him a suitable lady to propose to; for marriage is almost a *sine qua non* for worldly respectability.

Dipsychus dismisses the Spirit, in order to meditate, alone, on his advice. A legal career disgusts him; lawyers make their money out of the dirt in other people's lives. As for religion, perhaps the Spirit's message is not so different from that of *Qui Laborat, Orat*:

> *if indeed it be in vain*
> *To expect to find in this more modern time*
> *That which the old world styled, in old-world phrase,*
> *Walking with God. It seems His newer will*
> *We should not think of Him at all, but trudge it,*
> *And of the world He has assigned us make*
> *What best we can.*

(P: 268)

As for marriage, Dipsychus had hoped for something better than an arranged match. He had dreamed of a 'love, the large repose/ Restorative, not to mere outside needs skin-deep, but throughly to the total man'. But such love, though possible, is so rare that it is

> *A thing not possibly to be conceived*
> *An item in the reckonings of the wise.*

(P: 269)

But Dipsychus is reluctant to give up hope of a life of action. Rather than submit to the world, by taking up a career moulded by the existing institutions, he had hoped by some unprecedented and individual action to change the world for the better. The difficulty is in choosing the moment for such decisive action. If one leaps into the fray prematurely, one may court ignominious defeat; if one defers intervention too long, the opportunity for any contribution may go past. In eighty lines of grandiose blank verse, of uneven worth, Dipsychus weighs up the opposing dangers of precipitation and procrastination. Here are some of the better lines:

177

> *The dashing stream*
> *Stays not to pick his steps among the rocks*
> *Or let his water-breaks be chronicled.*
> *And though the hunter looks before he leap,*
> *'Tis instinct rather than a shaped-out thought*
> *That lifts him his bold way. Then, instinct, hail*
> *And farewell hesitation! If I stay*
> *I am not innocent; nor if I go –*
> *E'en should I fall – beyond redemption lost.*
>
> *Ah, if I had a course like a full stream,*
> *If life were as the field of chase! No, no;*
> *The age of instinct has, it seems, gone by*
> *And will not be forced back. And to live now*
> *I must sluice out myself into canals,*
> *And lose all force in ducts. The modern Hotspur*
> *Shrills not his trumpet of 'To Horse, To Horse!'*
> *But consults columns in a railway guide;*
> *A demigod of figures; an Achilles*
> *Of computation.*

(P: 271)

Worse, the modern world does not really leave room for individual action at all; everything is collective and anonymous, and the overall effect of the communal endeavour is unverifiable by those who contribute to it:

> *We ask Action,*
> *And dream of arms and conflict; and string up*
> *All self-devotion's muscles; and are set*
> *To fold up papers. To what end? We know not.*
> *Other folks do so; it is always done;*
> *And it perhaps is right. And we are paid for it.*
> *For nothing else we can be.*

(P: 272)

After some unquoted Napoleonic bombast, these staccato phrases mark the collapse of the blank verse – so eerily predictive of Clough's later service to Florence Nightingale, summed up in Lytton Strachey's notorious phrase 'parcels to be done up in brown paper, and carried to the post'.

If heroic action were possible, unselfish and yet individual, that would be a worthy aim in life; but Dipsychus now accepts that it is a romantic dream. In two resounding, image-packed stanzas he announces his submission. He believes that he has taken his decision alone; but his 'I submit' is at once echoed by the Spirit, off stage, and applauded in language which echoes the language and imagery of *Epi-Strauss-ion*:

> *Submit, submit!*
> *'Tis common sense, and human wit*
> *Can claim no higher name than it*
> *Submit, submit!*
>
> *Devotion, and ideas, and love,*
> *And beauty claim their place above;*
> *But saint and sage and poet's dreams,*
> *Divide the light in coloured streams,*
> *Which this alone gives all combined*
> *The siccum lumen of the mind*
> *Called common sense.*

(P. 272)

But now it is common sense, not divine revelation, which provides the dry white light which supersedes the stained glass of religion, philosophy, and poetry. The Spirit uses the biblical imagery of the Good Shepherd to welcome Dipsychus into the fold:

> *O did you think you were alone?*
> *That I was so unfeeling grown*
> *As not with joy to leave behind*
> *My ninety-nine in hope to find*
> *(How sweet the words my sense express)*
> *My lost sheep in the wilderness?*

In the eleventh scene, Dipsychus looks back over the life he is to leave, symbolized by Venice. The night scene in the piazza which he disdained at the beginning of part one is now lovingly described in richly textured blank verse, some of the finest in the poem. Not only is he now reconciled to the people and the architecture of the city; he can see something positive even in the temptations it presents:

> *What we call sin*
> *I could believe a painful opening out*
> *Of paths for ampler virtue . . .*
> *Was any change,*

> *Any now blest expansion, but at first*
> *A pang, remorse-like, shot to the inmost seats*
> *Of moral being? To do anything,*
> *Distinct on any one thing to decide,*
> *To leave the habitual and the old, and quit*
> *The easy chair of use and wont, seems crime*
> *To the weak soul, forgetful how at first*
> *Sitting down seemed so too.* (P: 274)

Dipsychus describes how in his previous life moods of despair and contentment have alternated:

> *Oh, there are hours,*
> *When love, and faith, and dear domestic ties,*
> *And converse with old friends, and pleasant walks,*
> *Familiar faces, and familiar books,*
> *Study, and art, upliftings unto prayer,*
> *And admiration of the noblest things,*
> *Seem all ignoble only: all is mean,*
> *And nought as I would have it. Then at others,*
> *My mind is on her nest; my heart at home*
> *In all around; my soul secure in place,*
> *And the vext needle perfect to her poles.* (P: 275)

The alternation of despair and hope is redescribed in Venetian images. Baffled wandering through byways is contrasted with the glorious survey from the Campanile's top. On workdays life is dull, the world weary; on the Lord's day Dipsychus is in the Spirit with John receiving his revelation in Patmos.

In Dipsychus's lines we can recognize a close-fitting description of Clough's own spiritual biography. But we can recognize it even more accurately when the Spirit, in an echo of Dipsychus's soliloquy, shows that for deflationary purposes he can use blank verse no less effectively than tetrameters:

> *O yes,*
> *To moon about religion; to inhume*
> *Your ripened age in solitary walks,*
> *For self-discussion; to debate in letters*
> *Vext points with earnest friends; past other men*
> *To cherish natural instincts, yet to fear them*
> *And less than any use them.* (P: 276)

He turns Dipsychus's Venetian imagery against him, to forestall
any backsliding from his resolve to face the world:

> *Stay at Venice, if you will;*
> *Sit musing in its churches hour on hour*
> *Cross-kneed upon a bench; climb up at whiles*
> *The neighbouring tower, and kill the lingering day*
> *With old comparisons; when night succeeds*
> *Evading, yet a little seeking, what*
> *You would and would not, turn your doubtful eyes*
> *On moon and stars to help morality*
> *Once in a fortnight say, by lucky chance*
> *Of happier-tempered coffee gain (great Heaven!)*
> *A pious rapture: it is not enough?*
> *O that will keep you safe. Yet don't be sure.*

(P: 276)

Dipsychus attempts to renege on his submission of the previous
scene, but the Spirit warns that unless he comes to terms with the
world, he is likely to fall into something worse:

> *Sink ere the end, most like, the hapless prey*
> *Of some chance chambermaid, more sly than fair,*
> *And in vain call for me.*

(P: 277)

Once again, the scene ends in submission to the mocking tones of
the Spirit:

> *Submit, submit*
> *As your good father did before you*
> *And as the mother who first bore you!*
> *O yes! a child of heavenly birth!*
> *But it was pupped too on earth.*
> *Keep your new birth for that far day*
> *When in the grave your bones you lay*
> *All with your kindred and connection*
> *In hopes of happy resurrection.*

(P: 278)

Neither Wordsworthian fancies of pre-existence, nor Christian
hopes of afterlife, should get in the way of living, here and now,
after the dictates of common sense.

181

The final scenes of the drama appear excessively drawn out. Of course the procrastination of Dipsychus is an essential part of his character; but it could be more effectively portrayed by making a selection of the best passages in which his hesitations and tergiversations are expressed. No doubt this is what, in a final revision, Clough would himself have carried out, had he ever decided to make the work public.

In any final revision, from scene 12 it would be important to keep the Spirit's self-characterization as

> *This compound of convention and impiety*
> *This mongrel of uncleanness and propriety*
>
> (P: 280)

and the wording of Dipsychus's now thrice repeated submission:

> *Welcome, wicked world*
> *The hardening heart, the calculating brain*
> *Narrowing its doors to thought, the lying lips*
> *The calm-dissembling eyes; the greedy flesh,*
> *The world, the Devil – welcome, welcome, welcome!*
>
> (P: 281)

But the main new element which is added by the scene is the Spirit's rejection of the possible alternatives which Dipsychus might hope to choose to save him from earning his living in the world: poetry, philosophy, teaching.

First, poetry. Dipsychus may no doubt continue to versify as in the gondola scene:

> *Be large of aspiration, pure in hope,*
> *Sweet in fond longings, but in all things vague.*
> *Breathe out your dreamy scepticism, relieved*
> *By snatches of old songs.*
>
> (P: 283)

People may like it, but will the world take notice? The Spirit is sceptical and ironical:

> *The strong fresh gale of life will feel, no doubt,*
> *The influx of your mouthful of soft air.*
>
> (P: 283)

Or will Dipsychus write about philosophy?

> *For a waste far-off* maybe *overlooking*
> *The fruitful* is *close by, live in metaphysic*
> *With transcendental logic fill your stomach,*
> *Schematise joy, effigiate meat and drink;*
> *Or, let me see, a mighty Work, a Volume*
> *The Complemental of the inferior Kant,*
> *The Critic of Pure Practic, based upon*
> *The Antinomies of the Moral Sense: for, look you*
> *We cannot act without assuming* x,
> *And at the same time* y *its contradictory.*
> *Ergo to act.*
>
> (P: 284)

But even if Dipsychus succeeds in out-Kanting Kant, will people really buy such works? Or will he try pupil-teaching, in spite of his unorthodox opinions which will make him suspect to parents?

> *Well, old college fame,*
> *The charity of some free-thinking merchant*
> *Or friendly intercession brings a first pupil*
> *But not a second.*
>
> (P: 284)

After these remarks, so very close to the bone of Clough's own experience, the Spirit points the way Dipsychus's life is leading:

> *Will you go on thus*
> *Until death end you? If indeed it does*
> *For what it does, none knows. Yet as for you*
> *You'll hardly have the courage to die outright;*
> *You'll somehow halve even it. Methinks I see you,*
> *Through everlasting limbos of void time,*
> *Twirling and twiddling ineffectively,*
> *And indeterminately swaying for ever.*
>
> (P: 284)

It is time for Dipsychus to grow up, to cease sucking at the dugs of instinct and open his mouth for spoon-meat. Indeed:

> *We'll put you up*
> *Into the higher form. 'Tis time you learn*
> *The Second Reverence, for things around.*
>
> (P: 284)

183

The scene which could most easily be spared from the final part of the poem is the brief scene 12. Dipsychus claims that he is succumbing to the Spirit only as a stratagem, treacherously planning to use the strength the Spirit gives to overcome the Spirit and his works. At the very least, he intends, like Samson, to bring down the Philistine world in a catastrophe which will destroy himself as well. Dipsychus's protestations do not convince the Spirit and are no doubt not meant to be found persuasive by the reader. None the less, the conception seems obstructive dramatically, and its execution, in the text now standard, is grossly imperfect.

Dipsychus first recalls a vision, recorded in a poem beginning 'When the enemy is near thee/ Call on us!' which is most charitably interpreted as a parody. He then describes and justifies his stratagem in a long series of overloaded images. The only memorable lines belong to a different line of thought. The theme of the previous scene was that acceptance of the world is the sign of maturity. This theme is now taken up again, with an appeal, familiar elsewhere in Clough's poetry, to the imagery of Genesis:

> *'The man his parents shall desert',*
> *The ordinance says, 'and cleave unto his wife.'*
> *O man, behold thy wife, the hard naked world;*
> *Adam, accept thy Eve.*

(P: 287)

The final scene begins with Dipsychus preparing to clinch his bargain with Mephisto; he is, after all, merely making friends with the Mammon of Unrighteousness. But will not the Spirit be satisfied with a portion merely of his soul – three-quarters, say, or even nine-tenths? Mephisto will be content with nothing less than the whole. But then Dipsychus rounds on him at last:

> *Yet know, Mephisto, know, nor you nor I*
> *Can in this matter either sell or buy . . .*
> *Oh, your soul chance was in the childish mind*
> *Whose darkness dreamed that vows like this could bind.*

(P: 289)

Mephisto is not disconcerted; time will show

> *Which of us two will closest fit*
> *The proverb of the Biter Bit.*

(P: 290)

The scene, and the poem, ends with a meditation on a passage in the Epistle to the Ephesians where the writer exhorts:

> Put on the whole armour of God, that ye may be able to stand against the wiles of the devil. For we wrestle not against flesh and blood, but against principalities, against powers, against the rulers of the darkness of this world, against spiritual wickedness in high places.
>
> (Ephesians 6: 11–12)

The Spirit accepts the description of himself as ruler of the world; he prefers the Greek name *kosmokrator* to any of the Hebrew names with which the Scriptures refer to the Devil. Dipsychus's last words, before going off with the Spirit to his new life, are:

> *Yet in all these things we – 'tis Scripture too –*
> *Are more than conquerors even over you.*
>
> (P: 291)

But it is the Spirit who really has the last word, by quoting a nursery rhyme:

> *Little Bo Peep, she lost her sheep*
> *And knew not where to find them.*

Silly Dipsychus has hitherto been one of Bo Peep's sheep; but now at last he has left the land of nursery rhyme. He has been taken into the fold of the Good Shepherd who is also the Ruler of this darkness.

EPILOGUE: THE DOUBLE MIND AND THE SINGLE HEART

Bernard Richards, in his anthology *English Verse 1830–1890*, wrote an essay introducing his selection of Clough's poems in which he made the comparison between Clough and Hopkins:

> There are analogies between C. and Hopkins. Their poetic outputs are not very large (though it should be remembered that C. wrote as much poetry as Arnold); they both died in early middle age; they both expressed a certain impatience with stilted poetic diction, and hoped for a revivification of poetry from colloquial sources: they both experimented with a prosody that took more account of stress than syllable; and their work was so bound up with their inner lives that it tended to 'live' for a long time as a developing organism, and then to be abandoned rather than finished and worked up for publication. So enormous responsibility has fallen on editorial midwives, and the poetry is perhaps best regarded as having a sort of provisional existence. This even applies in C.'s case to poetry published in his lifetime – such as *Amours* and *The Bothie*. . . . As with Hopkins, the earlier editors were inevitably more limited and conventional than the poet himself; this was true of his wife Blanche, of F. T. Palgrave, who wrote the introduction for *Poems* (1862) and even (though to a lesser extent) of J. Addington Symons, who assisted in the production of *Poems and Prose Remains* (1869).
>
> (Richards, *English Verse 1830–1890*: 290)

The comparison, as the present volume has shown, can be taken very much further. The education of the two men, reading classics and philosophy at Balliol, was almost exactly the same, despite the generation's gap between them. Both of them during their Oxford days came under the influence of the same people. Jowett, for instance, was a scholar senior to Clough and was the tutor of the undergraduate Hopkins; John Henry Newman fascinated Clough with his sermons, and guided Hopkins into the Roman Catholic Church with his advice.

Both men in their undergraduate days were regarded as persons of enormous promise; each, in his day, was described as being the most intelligent student at Balliol. Both men were regarded by the friends of their college days as having failed to live up to their promise. The stigma of failure, indeed, attached to both of them throughout their lives. Clough was an academic drop-out who was unable to find and keep any suitable job until he was thrust into one by his friends across the distance of an ocean. Hopkins was regarded by his Anglican friends as having thrown away his talents by becoming a Jesuit, and by his Jesuit colleagues as a difficult eccentric who was a misfit in each of the offices to which he was posted by the Society.

Both men were comparatively indifferent to reputation, and left much of their best poetry unpublished. Clough might well have endorsed the remarks of Hopkins in a letter to Dixon on the topic of fame:

> It is a great danger in itself, as dangerous as wealth every bit, I should think, and as hard to enter the kingdom of heaven with. . . . What I do regret is the loss of recognition belonging to the work itself. For as to every moral act, being right or being wrong, there belongs, of the nature of things, reward or punishment, so to every form perceived by the mind belongs, of the nature of things, admiration of the reverse. . . .
>
> Nevertheless fame whether won or lost is a thing which lies in the award of a random, reckless, incompetent and unjust judge, the public, the multitude.
>
> (L, II: 7)

In each of the two poets this indifference to fame went hand in hand with a firm confidence in his own poetic talent. Each was unperturbed by severe criticism from friends highly qualified as judges of verse. Thus Hopkins was unshaken by Bridges's hostile reaction to *The Wreck of the Deutschland*, and Clough was not downcast when Arnold told him that *Amours de Voyage* did not suit him (Lowry: 132).

Both poets, as Richards remarked, made an effort to avoid stilted diction and artificially heightened poetic style. Thus Hopkins, as he wrote to Bridges in 1879, deliberately avoided inversion, because it had an enfeebling effect:

> So also I cut myself off from the use of *ere, o'er, wellnigh, what time, say not* (for *do not say*) because, though dignified, they neither belong to nor could ever arise from, or be the elevation of, ordinary modern speech.
>
> (L, I: 89)

This rule would condemn many lines of Clough's poetry, and would indeed damn from the outset his most famous poem ('Say not the struggle naught availeth'). But though Clough did have a number of irritating mannerisms, such as the frequent use of 'e'er' and 'ah', Hopkins at times shares them (as in the last line of *God's Grandeur*: 'the Holy Ghost over the bent/ world broods with warm breast and with ah! bright wings'). Hopkins may have avoided noun–verb inversion, but he is all too fond of adjective–article inversion as in 'wisest my heart' and 'mortal my mate'. Despite Hopkins's anxiety to capture in verse the register of common and informal speech, a line of his poems could almost never be mistaken for a spontaneous conversational utterance. Whereas Clough showed himself capable of producing natural conversational diction in a variety of idioms, such as the Oxford slang as well as the Scots dialect in *The Bothie*.

Many more similarities may be traced between the education, thought, and poetic theory of Clough and Hopkins. But in spite of all this, would it not be absurd to compare the two together as craftsmen? Is not Hopkins incomparably the greater poet?

If, in a poet, what we most admire is the craftsmanship of the verse then there can be no question that Hopkins far outshines Clough. Clough is the more versatile poet, and can show successful ventures in many different poetic genres; but in every one of these genres which Hopkins too has set his hand to, he achieves much more powerful effects.

If, however, we judge a poet also by the quality of his thought, and his skill in casting light on the nature of human existence in the world, it is not clear to me that Hopkins so clearly outclasses Clough. We can identify three major areas where we may look to a poet for enlightenment: the world of nature, the world of human relations, and the world of the spirit. In the first of these areas, Hopkins is clearly superior; in the second Clough equally clearly has the mastery. In the third case, it is no simple matter to award the palm.

In the description of natural beauty Hopkins is unequalled not only by Clough but by any other poet writing in English. In Clough's poems, and especially in *The Bothie*, there are many agreeable descriptions of scenery; throughout his work there are telling images drawn from the natural world. But there is nothing to compare with Hopkins's gift for capturing a colour, a pattern, an animal motion, a complicated natural process, in a brief, unforgettable phrase.

When we turn from nature to society, the situation is reversed. Human relations are very rarely the theme of Hopkins's poetry, and the only natural relationship between human beings which he was able convincingly to render in verse was fraternal comradeship, as in *Brothers*. Clough, on the other hand, can make the reader enter into a great variety of relationships between human beings in different kinds of encounter.

The contrast between the two poets in this matter emerges most clearly if we compare their treatment of women. Hopkins's account of Adam and Eve, and his view of the nature of marriage, emphasized the subjection of women. In the index of his spiritual writings there is no entry for 'women', and under 'woman' only a reference to 'woman of the Apocalypse'. Only the Virgin Mary and the Virgin Martyrs provide themes of femininity for his mature verses.

Clough, on the other hand, could describe in masterly fashion relationships between the sexes of many kinds, from the most transitory to the most enduring. There is the elemental sympathy expressed by the faint stirring of mutual sexual attraction in a chance encounter in a railway carriage, in *Natura Naturans*. There is the solicitation and rebuff of the prostitute in *Dipsychus*. There is the scandalized rejection by a woman of an improper approach at a party in the early poem 'False words they were'. (Is that, like so many of Clough's poems, based on an event in his own life, a rebuff to some clumsy wooing of his own?) There is the breathless romantic passion of *Epi Latmo* – the progress from disdain to infatuation via juxtaposition in *Amours de Voyage* – and there is the long, endearing account of the wooing and the wedding which concludes *The Bothie*. The young, unmarried Clough can even, in *The Bothie*, capture quiet moods of middle-aged connubial tenderness, as when he describes how a man may be moved by noticing the altered gait of his pregnant wife. Clough's love poetry deserves to have a whole book devoted to it.

It is with the third area, the area of the spirit, that this book has been concerned. Here a reader's view of the comparative merits of Hopkins and Clough as poetic thinkers is likely to be coloured by his own religious position: believers will be more inclined to praise Hopkins, and unbelievers to praise Clough. Few, however, are likely to identify wholly with one or the other. Even the most enthusiastic Catholic, after the second Vatican Council, will find it hard to accept some of the more exuberant aspects of Hopkins's devotions, and the degree of intransigence he displays in regard to non-Catholic piety and virtue. On the other hand, few agnostics today would share the extremely sceptical view which Clough took of the historicity of the Christian Gospels.

Hopkins, praising the nun drowning in the *Deutschland*, says: 'Ah, there was a heart right/ There was single eye.' The description 'single eye' would apply to himself; he saw many things very clearly, but he never saw more than one side of any question. Clough, like his own Dipsychus, could see two sides to every question; in this sense he was the most double-minded of men.

Clough's most successful attempt, in prose, to state fairly the two sides to the question of Christian belief comes in a paper of uncertain date, first published posthumously, entitled 'Notes on the Religious Tradition':

> It is impossible for any scholar to have read, and studied, and reflected without forming a strong impression of the entire uncertainty of history in general, and of the history of Christianity in particular.
>
> It is equally impossible for any man to live, act, and reflect without feeling the significance and the depth of the moral and religious teaching which passes amongst us by the name of Christianity.
>
> The more a man feels the value, the true import of this, the more will he hesitate to base it upon those foundations which as a scholar he feels to be unstable. Manuscripts are doubtful, records may be unauthentic, criticism is feeble, historical facts must be left uncertain. Even in like manner my own personal experience is most limited, perhaps even most delusive; what have I seen, what do I know? Nor is my personal judgement a thing which I feel any great satisfaction in trusting. My reasoning powers are weak; my memory doubtful and confused; my conscience, it may be, callous and vitiated.
>
> (PPR, 1: 422)

In this predicament, Clough says, a sane and humble-minded man must throw himself upon the great religious tradition. This does not mean accepting that everything in the Gospel narrative is an essential integral part of the tradition; nor does it mean, ignoring scientific and historical doubts, 'to take refuge in Romish infalli-bility, and, to avoid sacrificing the four Gospels, consent to accept the legends of the saints and the tales of modern miracles'.

It is conceivable that God has given us a reason which is unreliable when it comes to matters of faith:

> The rule which he has placed to measure all things by and bid us trust in them implicitly may be, by His special purpose, false for the highest things. What in our solemn courts of justice we should call false witness, may be in the Church to decide our verdict; what in the exchange would be imposture, may be in the sanctuary pure truth. I say, this thing is conceivable; yet it is conceivable also that sense and mind, that intellect and religious, things without and things within, are in harmony with each other.

What seems most likely is that religious truths of the highest import grow up naturally, but come to us involved in uncertain traditions, encrusted by accessory legends. We must digest these traditions, separating the nutritive portion from the innutritive:

> It may be true that man has fallen, though Adam and Eve are legendary. It may be a divine fact that God is a person, and not a sort of natural force; and it may have happened that the tales of His personal appearance to Abraham, Isaac, and Jacob, were the means of sustaining and conveying down to posterity that belief, and yet that He never sat in the tent on the plains of Mamre, nor wrestled with Jacob by night, nor spoke with Moses in the mount.

In seeking to learn from the religious tradition, one should not restrict the field of one's search, but look everywhere:

> Everywhere – to India, if you will, and the ancient Bhagvad-Gita and the laws of Menu; to Persia and Hafiz; to China and Confucius; to the Vedas and the Shasters; to the Koran; to pagan Greece and Rome; to Homer; to Socrates and Plato; to Lucretius, to Virgil, to Tacitus. Try all things, I do not imagine that any spiritual doctrine or precept of life found in all that travel from east to west and north to south will disqualify us to return to what *prima facie* does appear to

be, not indeed the religion of the majority of mankind, but
the religion of the best, so far as we can judge in part history,
and despite of professed infidelity, of the most enlightened
of our own time.

It is true that each of us is born within a particular community of the
religious tradition; it is true that to a certain extent we must all of us
be of the religion of our fathers; we are so whether we like it or not,
whether we say we are, or say we are not. But that does not mean
that we cannot learn from other strands of the tradition. The
Protestant should not shut himself off from what he can learn from
the Catholic, nor the Unitarian reject the education offered by the
Episcopalian:

> [S]trive as I will, I am restricted, and grasp as I may I can
> never hold the complete truth. But that does not the least
> imply that I am justified in shutting the eyes of my under-
> standing to the facts of science, or its ears to the criticisms of
> history, nor yet in neglecting those pulsations of spiritual
> instinct which come to me from association at one time
> with Unitarians, at another with Calvinists, or again with
> Episcopalians and Roman Catholics. . . .
>   And it appears to me that it is much more the apparent
> dispensation of things that we should gradually widen, than
> that we should narrow and individualise our creeds. Why
> are we daily coming more and more into communication
> with each other, if it be not that we learn each other's
> knowledge and combine all into one?
>
> (PPR, 1: 425–6)

'Notes on the Religious Tradition' is an agreeably irenic pamphlet. Not only agnostics who feel the attraction of religion, but
Christian ecumenists at the present day, might feel they could adopt
much of it as a manifesto. Its wide tolerance is not, of course, typical
of every period of Clough's life; for that we may be thankful, since
otherwise we could have lost some of his finest satirical verse.

What would Clough and Hopkins have thought of each other?
The two men never met, and Hopkins was only a schoolboy when
Clough died. There is no reference to Clough in Hopkins's correspondence, and Jesuit libraries were unlikely to contain his
works. Certainly, in *Amours de Voyage*, Clough places in Claude's
mouth some crude anti-Jesuit polemic. Claude complains that in
Roman churches everything is:

Epilogue

Overlaid of course with infinite gauds and gewgaws,
Innocent, playful follies, the toys and trinkets
  of childhood,
Forces on maturer years as the serious one thing needful
By the barbarian will of the rigid and ignorant Spaniard.

Luther's reformation, Claude says, was a terrible mistake. The Renaissance was clearing out Romish superstitions and abuses; but Luther's 'huge Wittenberg lungs' brought back theology in a flood upon Europe which is hardly yet abated:

Luther, they say, was unwise; he didn't see how things were going;
Luther was foolish – but, O great God! what call you Ignatius?
O my tolerant soul, be still! but you talk of barbarians,
Alaric, Attila, Genseric; – why they came, they killed, they
Ravaged and went on their way; but these vile, tyrannous Spaniards,
These are here still, – how long, O ye heavens, in the country of
  Dante?
These, that fanaticized Europe, which now can forget them, release not
This, their choicest of prey, this Italy; here you see them; –
Here, with emasculate pupils and gimcrack curches of Gesù,
Pseudo-learning and lilies, confessional boxes and postures, –
Here, with metallic beliefs and regimental devotions, –
Here, overcrusting with slime, perverting, defacing, debasing,
Michael Angelo's dome, that had hung the Pantheon in heaven,
Raphael's joys and Graces, and thy clear stars, Galileo.

(P: 97)

It would be rash to assume that whatever Claude says expresses an opinion to which Clough himself would subscribe. But while many of the early, arrogant, puppyish judgements made by Claude are later discounted, this one remains unrecanted.

One wants to say to Claude, as Hopkins did to Bridges (L, I: 40): 'You say you don't like Jesuits. Did you ever see one?' But if Clough could not find it in his heart to sympathize with the Counter-Reformation, Hopkins is as merciless to the heroes of the Reformation itself. Luther in the *Deutschland* is 'beast of the waste wood' and bears the mark of Cain.

Perhaps Hopkins, had he read Clough, would have applied to him the remarks that he made about Matthew Arnold in a letter of 1873:

He seems a very earnest man and distinctly seeing the difference between jest and earnest and a master in both. . . . But then very unhappily he jokes at the wrong things, as I see from a very profane passage quoted from his new book; however that passage though profane is not blasphemous, for we are obliged to think of God by human thoughts and his account of them is substantially true.

(L, III: 58)

We may note finally one special feature of Clough's agnosticism. It is often said that an agnostic must go backward or forward, either into atheism or into religion. The editor of *Macmillan's Magazine* in an article on Clough's poems in August 1862 (pp. 318 ff.) says that Clough's own agnosticism is a refutation of this idea:

On the contrary, a kind of resigned and humble satisfaction with the speculative state as the truest attainable, a kind of jealous watchfulness lest he should be lured or driven out of it, a kind of resolution never to go backward or forward from it, and to regard all promises of more definite certainty inducing him to do either as temptations of evil – that is what we see in Clough.

(Vol. vi, 1862: 325)

There is something paradoxical about the state of a man who thus resists the resolution of a question which above all others torments him. But none knew this better than Clough himself; and he wrote in one of his notebooks a brief verse that could well stand as his own epitaph:

> *To spend uncounted years of pain,*
> *Again, again, and yet again,*
> *In working out in heart and brain*
> *The problem of our being here;*
> *To gather facts from far and near*
> *Upon the mind to hold them clear*
> *And, knowing more may yet appear,*
> *Unto one's latest breath to fear*
> *The premature result to draw –*
> *Is this the object, end, and law*
> *And purpose of our being here?*

(P: 313)

BIBLIOGRAPHICAL NOTE

Details of the editions of the poetry and prose of Clough and Hopkins used for quotations in this study appear in the list of Abbreviations on page xvii.

A comprehensive bibliographical guide to works by and about Clough appeared in 1968: Gollin, Richard M., Houghton, Walter E., and Timko, Michael, *Arthur Hugh Clough, a Descriptive Catalogue*, The New York Public Library. This is annotated, and is divided into three parts; Poetry, Prose, Biography and Criticism; the critical section contains 500 items.

Books on Clough which I have found particularly useful in writing this book include:

Biswas, R. K., *Arthur Hugh Clough: Towards a Reconsideration*, Oxford, 1972.

Chorley, Katherine, *Arthur Hugh Clough: the Uncommitted Mind*, Oxford, 1962.

Greenberger, E. B., *Arthur Hugh Clough: the Growth of a Poet's Mind*, Harvard, 1970.

Houghton, Walter E., *The Poetry of Clough: an Essay in Revaluation*, New Haven, 1963.

Lowry, H. F., *The Letters of Matthew Arnold to Arthur Hugh Clough*, Oxford, 1932.

Thorpe, Michael (Ed.) *Clough, the Critical Heritage*, New York, 1982.

Timko, Michael, *Innocent Victorian: the Satiric Poetry of Arthur Hugh Clough*, Ohio, 1966.

The most recent bibliography of Hopkins is by Dunne, Tom, *Gerard Manley Hopkins: A Comprehensive Bibliography*, Oxford, 1976.

Many volumes of biography and criticism of Hopkins have been written. I single out a very few which illuminate aspects of his work discussed in the present book:

Gardner, W. H., *Gerard Manley Hopkins, 1844–1889: A Study of Poetic Idiosyncrasy in Relation to Poetic Tradition*, 2 vols., second edition, London, 1948.

Kitchen, Paddy, *Gerard Manley Hopkins*, London, 1978.

Keating, J. E. *'The Wreck of the Deutschland': An Essay and Commentary*, Kent, Ohio, 1963.

McKenzie, Norman H., *A Reader's Guide to Gerard Manley Hopkins*, London, 1981.

Peters, W. A. M., *Gerard Manley Hopkins: A Critical Essay towards the Understanding of his Poetry*, Oxford, 1970.

Pick, John, *Gerard Manley Hopkins: Priest and Poet*, London, 1966.

Sulloway, Allison G., *Gerard Manley Hopkins and the Victorian Temper*, London, 1972.

Thomas, Alfred, *Hopkins the Jesuit*, London, 1969.

Other works referred to in the text are:

Kenny, Anthony, *The Legacy of Wittgenstein*, Oxford, 1984.

Newman, John Henry, *Parochial and Plain Sermons*, London, 1868.

Apologia pro Vita Sua, ed. M. Svaglic, Oxford, 1967.

Ricks, Christopher, (Ed.), *The New Oxford Book of Victorian Verse*, Oxford, 1987.

Ward, Wilfrid, *William George Ward and the Oxford Movement*, London, 1889.

INDEX